MW00938910

HEAVEN AND THE IN-BETWEEN

What Happens after We Die through the Eyes of a Medium

Marnie Hill

BALBOA.PRESS

A DIVISION OF HAY HOUSE

Copyright © 2019 Marnie Hill.

All rights reserved. No part of this book may be used or reproduced by any means, graphic, electronic, or mechanical, including photocopying, recording, taping or by any information storage retrieval system without the written permission of the author except in the case of brief quotations embodied in critical articles and reviews.

Balboa Press books may be ordered through booksellers or by contacting:

Balboa Press
A Division of Hay House
1663 Liberty Drive
Bloomington, IN 47403
www.balboapress.com
1 (877) 407-4847

Because of the dynamic nature of the Internet, any web addresses or links contained in this book may have changed since publication and may no longer be valid. The views expressed in this work are solely those of the author and do not necessarily reflect the views of the publisher, and the publisher hereby disclaims any responsibility for them.

The author of this book does not dispense medical advice or prescribe the use of any technique as a form of treatment for physical, emotional, or medical problems without the advice of a physician, either directly or indirectly. The intent of the author is only to offer information of a general nature to help you in your quest for emotional and spiritual well-being. In the event you use any of the information in this book for yourself, which is your constitutional right, the author and the publisher assume no responsibility for your actions.

Any people depicted in stock imagery provided by Getty Images are models, and such images are being used for illustrative purposes only. Certain stock imagery © Getty Images.

Print information available on the last page.

ISBN: 978-1-9822-3781-3 (sc)
ISBN: 978-1-9822-3783-7 (hc)
ISBN: 978-1-9822-3782-0 (e)

Library of Congress Control Number: 2019917442

Balboa Press rev. date: 01/21/2020

CONTENTS

Marnie shares with you her knowledge and experiences regarding her encounters with the spirit world, the soul, and the importance of her walk with Jesus Christ.

All situations have been altered so that no resemblance to persons living or dead may be identified to a specific case, reading, or example that is being discussed within the book.

"Through our pain, God shapes us. He moulds us into His image so we can serve the greater purpose of His Creation." Marnie Hill

INTRODUCTION

Let me take a moment to introduce myself and explain why you should even listen to what I have to say. I was born with the ability to speak with the afterlife. Ever since I can remember, I have had spiritual experiences. From the time I began offering medium readings to my clients, I've learned that there seems to be a universal experience regarding life after death. Some people have had the opportunity to see their loved ones after they've passed, while others have endured unusual paranormal experiences featuring ghosts or angelic encounters. There's something genuine happening within the unseen realms that the human world can and has experienced. However, many who have had these experiences seem to be afraid to share their stories. Perhaps they're scared of being misunderstood, looked upon as crazy, or fearful that their loved ones will not believe them, so many choose to remain quiet.

It seems these experiences occur at various times throughout our lives, especial after a loss of a loved that seems to bring forward a large amount of healing to the recipient. These might be experiences with angels that have saved lives and brought healing, fearful experiences that seem to awaken us to the possibility of a hostile unseen world, or spiritual lessons of a deity that either brings immediate change or gradually transforms the human soul. My personal experiences have led me on the road to healing and made me aware of the need to understand my skills and abilities as a medium.

I believe that some of my experiences have felt like miracles, but I guess that would be a meaning that's in the eye of the beholder.

Some of my experiences have been unusual, while some spiritual encounters were downright strange. My encounters with the spiritual realms led to me becoming a truth seeker of spirit. My desire to understand and to bring light to the religious elements that have presented themselves to me from the other side has empowered me to keep searching and to understand everything clearly. As a truth seeker, I'm a spiritual explorer. I've allowed many doors to open from the other side and quickly learned which doors I should not open and which ones were okay to open. Within this book I will reveal all of my knowledge to date.

My goal with this book is to help and inform people about the reality regarding life after death and provide others with information that would enable them to a better life experience. I've learned many lessons on this spiritual path, lessons I need to share. The dearly departed have revealed many things to me, the information about which the angels have offered advice have changed me, but my walk with Jesus Christ transformed me. My experiences remind me of the importance of living happier, the power of forgiveness, and the value of prayer. I've also learned about the significance of death. I've experienced good spirits, evil spirits, and the Holy One, whom I call Jesus.

While I mention Jesus Christ, rest assured that this isn't a religious book. I don't consider this a sacred text or a book about Christianity. This book is about faith and about believing and allowing. When I talk about heaven, my information comes from a place of truth and love. You'll hear about my past experiences and where these have led me today. My drive to understand my gift is as real as it is strong. I've seen the dark and one day I had to awaken to the realization that when you walk in darkness, it's only then that you finally learn how to embrace the light.

Over the years, I've experienced pain and misfortune and have learned each has a purpose. However, it took me years to truly understand that my spiritual quest for purpose wasn't about me, even though I was going through the heartache and experiencing the pain from others. In essence, it was all about Jesus. All of my experiences, whether good or bad, required me to look inside my heart and soul and each time I did, I always found Him. My search for ways to understand my pain led me back to Jesus, every time and with Him I found peace.

I've learned that death is simply a doorway that allows us to go home. Throughout life, we learn how to get back to God and this is our quest in life. Your journey is love. For me to understand my path as a medium and my experiences, I had to learn how I could trust it. I had to follow its will, which was the will of God. That was a journey in itself and not one I wish to endure again.

In this book, you'll find that on many occasions I interchange the words, heaven, the other side, and the afterlife. They all mean the same thing to me but after my experiences, I prefer to use the word heaven as the ultimate place for our soul. The place I call the in-between is not a place in heaven but somewhere that resides halfway between our world and the next, or heaven. I even briefly examine the lowest level that exists on the other side. I refer to this place as either the lower level or may use the word hell. I've never seen fire and a man with horns and a pitchfork in the lower levels. However, I have seen something and someone very close to this description. Evil does walk the earth. I do believe in Satan. When it comes to expressing the word God that is what resonates with me. However, the words source or Creator may be what resonate with you. I don't wish to dictate to you and am merely sharing my own experiences to help you.

Our world is changing, and indeed it needs to change, but we can never forget that it all started with love and it all began with God. We're all children of the high and mighty or the big guy upstairs, as one spirit once called God during one of my readings. I'm pretty sure the deceased person in that particular reading was also trying to get a laugh out of us. He wanted to break the tension or fear one may have during the course of a medium reading. He explained this to me and I then retold the story to his daughter. I explained that her dad just pointed up to the sky and mentioned the big guy upstairs. She laughed and said that was her dad, who had called God the big guy upstairs all the time. Everyone seems to have some sort of unique name for God and I personally feel this has everything to do with our personal reflection of what God represents to each of us. Jesus' spirit is compelling to me and I often feel His love and light during a medium reading. His energy flows into my own life when He seems to know when I need Him the most.

The Holy Spirit is an immense and powerful force that comes from God Himself and is unique, yet not separate from, Jesus. All three are intertwined with no ending and no beginning. It just is and it is one with God. When you experience the Holy Spirit, it takes you, changes you, and it can be addicting. It's the best spiritual experience I have ever had. I'm not kidding! The Holy Spirit is available to all of us that want this light to enter into their world. The energy source seems to be different for many of us. You can also deny this source of light if you so choose. I hope you can see the effects it has had on my life and in my writings throughout this book. I believe the extreme calmness or peace that flows within each of us could very well be the Holy Spirit coming directly from the spiritual realms. Some may give other names to their experiences and feelings and that's perfectly okay too.

The angels have consistently told me crucial information about heaven, speaking with the deceased, and life within the unseen worlds. There is a heaven and it has different levels and different names for different people. Top-level, the place with God, is where every soul strives to reach and this is why living our life now is so essential. We all have soul lessons that each one of us needs to learn within our human lifetime. If we don't learn them on Earth, many will discover it within heaven, while many may not. If people don't make such discoveries this is because some lessons that one must understand and obey within our world cannot be changed.

The choices you make today and how you view your pain are essential to your soul's growth. I like to say that you have opportunities in life. You can dwell on the past and that has no energy as the past no longer exists. You can concentrate on positively viewing your experiences as soul lessons that you needed to encounter, learn from, forgive then move on. With each encounter or soul lesson, a person can learn how to embrace their teaching with gratitude, which in turn will allow their soul to become stronger from the experience. This creates an armour of love around you, equipped with a protective force no one can break, not even evil.

Our purpose in life is to learn how to be closer to God, not one with God since that is impossible but to be with Him. Learn to walk with Him and be beside Him. In essence, to become one with Him.

Some levels within heaven are like classrooms for the soul, a place for healing, and some are like cold and empty rooms you would find in a jail, which feels like hell to me. Heaven and hell, which is the lower level, are two very different places or scales. Try not to live your life thinking that you will fix everything when you finally die. It may not happen and you may not get that chance. Finding God may not save you, serving Him will. And this lesson is hard for many people, especially in the chaotic world in which we live.

You may not go to the place or the level you desire right after you pass if you haven't learned your soul lesson when you were alive. You will go to a level that matches your soul. However, if you work hard enough at life today, I believe change is possible. You can heal so when you pass your soul is in the safest place of all. Healing that takes place for your soul after death is a choice and this choice is with God and you.

Angels do exist within heaven and they do come to Earth and visit. However, they work for God, not for us. I will talk about angels in this book. Since they don't work for us, this means that we should in no way demand that they bring forward information or ask anything of them. Angels show up when God needs them to do His work. We can see the stories of angels within the Bible. These were written to inform us about them and these are biblical angels. It took me years to finally understand this truth. I have had visitations from angels and they have shown up to help me at devastating times in my life.

Throughout this book, you'll hear me talk about a place called the in-between. My spiritual team in heaven gave this word to me.

The in-between place is also the place where I carefully open the door to a certain level that is within heaven where spirit communication is connected and allowed for universal purpose. I use prayer before I talk to any deceased loved one and a sacred symbol that was a gift from the angel who watches over me, my guardian angel, Isabelle. This symbol is to be placed and used before a reading, so I can safely open the doorway to heaven. I was told to never provide or give this symbol to any other soul, unless I am given permission from my angel to do so. It's to help me and keep me safe from negative energy within these different realms. While I've always felt safe using the symbol, I also began to question why I needed this sacred symbol in the first place. All has been revealed to me in time.

During my journey with spirit, I have learned that demons are real, as is negative energy within the spirit realms and in the physical world.

Negative energy is everywhere and can adversely impact your life if you let it. This is because of free will, which is one of the spiritual laws God has given to all, even the darker realms, and something He will not take away. I believe God will not take this away as we need to have balance within this world, which means the light and the dark must both exist. If the dark didn't exist we wouldn't be able to grow and that is our purpose. This is why evil exists, since we grow from the experience. I also have the ability of spiritual discernment. Having the ability to distinguish between good and evil spirits has helped me immensely. I am a firm believer that if you're unable to distinguish between a good and evil spirit, you should probably not contact the dead or even request information from heaven, the other side. How will you know what spirit is speaking with you? I'm a firm believer that a true medium is born with the gift of mediumship. All you need to learn is an understanding of what kind of medium you are, have some rules about mediumship, learn about spiritual healing and spiritual energy, believe in a higher power of light, and only use your ability for good. This means that you do it from the heart, not the mind. The mind will take you into the ego. If you are a medium that's of the light, the spirit world will not only work with you, it will teach you.

Throughout this book, you will see why my belief about evil is genuine. I do not seek it. I don't hunt evil and I don't try to stir things up in the spiritual realm either. It's part of a domain and I can see all the different ones, enabling me to inform others. Unfortunately, people in the world and other spirit communicators, including mediums, avoid speaking about the reality of what sits within the realms of heaven or in the spirit world. Many avoid it at all costs and I can see why. There's so much anger in the world. Everyone claims that their god or law is correct and many deny the truth. Some feel it's too scary. It makes some people feel uncomfortable. After all, it's human nature to avoid what's fearful to us, what we can't explain, or what we are unable to control. The devil wants all of us to believe he isn't real. What a playground Satan could have if we thought the devil wasn't real and more like a mythical creature made up to scare us. I do know that I can do what I do and I see what I see. This is all part of my life purpose. I feel eternally grateful that it takes a lot to scare me. I absolutely love horror shows and evil doesn't frighten me. I have a spiritual team walking with me, protecting me from the other side. I will tell you about my personal experiences and while they're a little unusual, they are very real.

Over the years, I've learned that there's a price for everything we say, think, and do. I wouldn't be much of a communicator if I chose not to share everything with you, the good, the bad, and the downright ugly things. Within these pages I also share some of my spiritual secrets with you, to help you maintain daily love and peace within your life, no matter what you may be experiencing or the pain you have gone through during your time here on Earth. Some days I feel God has called me into a ministry, just not a conventional one. I approach everything I do now with love, truth, and with Jesus as my primary teacher. Actually, when I have a question for myself, I usually ask what Jesus would do.

I'm also going to talk about some important messages that have been brought forward to me within my readings. Talking to spirits should never be taken lightly. You always want to make sure your communication is from the light and your intention to have a reading is for healing. If your purpose or plan isn't of the highest for all involved, communication shuts off in the afterlife and the deceased may stop speaking altogether. Spirits in the afterlife know the spiritual laws and you'll also recognize some of them after reading this book.

My belief in Jesus Christ is strong. Actually, it's unbreakable. Many have tried to put a dent in it, without success. The Bible is open to interpretation and is one of the most controversial books ever written. The writing in the New Testament seems to change drastically after Jesus Christ of Nazareth died on the cross compared to the Old Testament. God became kinder or did He? Many things changed after that moment. Interestingly, God seemed more human after the resurrection. Is it because God is Jesus and felt the pain of the civilized world? Or is it because God grieved for His only son? I'm not sure and will leave that up to you to decide. I do believe the Bible is a living document for life. It changes as we change yet the words and meanings stay the same. I found that when I reread scripture, I experienced a new sense of the message. The Gospels showed me a different way to view what I was currently going through and this is why I'm so passionate about being a medium.

Never feel you are unworthy of receiving His love, no matter what. The way I see it, rules have been placed within our world, within the Bible to protect our planet and us, and teachings are brought forward to guide us.

As a medium, I take my work very seriously. I know how much healing can come from having faith and learning about God and His truth for all of us. I'm also very aware that mediums and psychics were called upon and valued in ancient times. They were called oracles, seers, prophets, priestess, or priests and were needed. Their services were used in a holy way, not like it is today. I don't delve too deeply into the ancient text and the times or speculate regarding when I believe the Bible changed, as this is not important for this book. I know and believe that what I do is not against God's will, if conducted in the right way.

CHAPTER ONE

~

Being A Medium

Some days, I feel like I'm living my life with one foot in heaven. When I attended my first class as an introduction to social work at the age of twenty-three, a light went on or you could say I had my 'aha' moment, after spending years overcoming my losses and disappointments in life. During one of the classes, we talked about what was normal or how one could define what was normal in one's life. I concluded that we couldn't describe what normal is, only what it is for ourselves. Everyone has their views and values, so how can we determine what is normal if, for some reason, normal isn't normal for another person. We have our perceptions regarding life and our own uniqueness about ourselves. In this book, I will not be discussing mental health issues regarding spiritual encounters, visions, hearing voices, or seeing apparitions. Neither will I be discussing what the Diagnostic and Statistical Manual of Mental Disorders, or DSM, says in relation to these experiences or about specific diseases. When it comes right down to it, some things are unexplainable and most spiritual or paranormal encounters aren't usually connected to a mental health disorder. Some may be, but there aren't many examples. A healthy person might have some very unusual abilities and think they are crazy, but they are completely sane! Someone may have an ability others can't explain then judgement is passed on them when others are afraid of what they can do. Sometimes we don't have an understanding or an explanation of certain skills or gifts, like the ability to talk to the dead. And then you have the people who are suffering from mental health issues and their spiritual experiences may correlate with their diagnosis.

I mention this because I didn't really understand what I was experiencing at an early age and I worried too that something might not be okay. Yet the spirit world kept telling me it was okay, so I felt okay. Imagine if you're having spiritual encounters and experiences and are so scared to tell someone. Your fear could send you into a downward spiral and fill your life with anxiety and depression if you allow it. This never happened to me personally, but I can see how easy it could happen to someone else. I've always felt different with what I can do and it took me years to learn how to harness my feelings, abilities, and empathic gifts. This is why I took such an interest in learning about mental health when I was younger. My education helped me find a place within my mind where I felt comfortable to be me and to be honest, feeling comfortable speaking about it. Believe me, I am still a little quiet and shy with regards to telling everyone about my encounters with the spirit world. I'm not sure I'll get over that one and I've come to terms with this.

As a physical medium and an empath, I feel other people's pain, the pain of the spirit world. Of course, I feel their happiness but also feel the pain of our society. This is painful at times. Sometimes life is scary for me. Stepping outside my home always requires me to take a deep breath and sometimes a prayer goes along with it. Believe me, I don't stay home very often. I love experiencing all that life has to offer. It isn't easy being an empath, since I can also feel what other people are thinking about me. If there's something about me they don't like, it hits me right away. This can make life a little uncomfortable at times. Thoughts hold power, thoughts are energy, and the mind can read thoughts. This type of energy turns into emotions, which any intuitive person can pick up on. This energy can be poisonous to an empath. However, you must remember that no one has power over you. You need to control your thoughts and perceptions and make sure that negative energy doesn't get the best of you. As a medium I tend to see the world differently and I am glad that I do. My empathic ability allows me to know immediately and intuitively when someone is lying or when their intentions are not of the light. This gift has helped me and the spirit world immensely with spirit communication and in my everyday life.

I was doing a reading for a woman and at the end of one of my conversations, I asked her if it sounded normal. I wasn't sure why I asked that question or in that way. It was probably because I'd been consumed with what is normal and what others think as normal. My client looked at me and declared that nothing about the situation was normal, but she completely understood what her loved one was saying. We laughed. It was funny at the time. Talking to people that have passed on can seem a little weird, but this is very typical for me. Who would have believed the healing that came from that incident. I learned very quickly to never again ask if things sounded normal in a reading.

I've always said that mediumship is a gift for the living and the deceased. However, it's also a gift to the receiver if adequately honoured and can feel like a curse only when misunderstood or not acknowledged. Throughout my journey, and as a result of all the lives I have touched, at some point in time I found me on my journey. Finding me was a powerful thing, but it didn't happen overnight. I had to surrender to Jesus before all would be revealed. I do believe this path, the path of a medium, is one of service and also a sacred path. It brought me even closer to God and can bring others closer to Him too, if one chooses for this to be so. I have always been close to God, desiring Him to come closer to me. But God works in mysterious ways and sometimes it may leave one feeling a little confused. That may be God's will too. Believe it or not, my spiritual experiences, my gift to talk to the other side, did actually bring me closer to Him. Something happens to your soul when you're reading for people in heaven. Franky, I don't know what I would do if I couldn't feel Jesus' divine spirit in my life. I think life would be complicated for me, since I feel normal with Jesus in my life.

You will see in this book how Jesus kept showing up in my life. I'm not sure if it was Jesus Christ or the Holy Spirit that was bringing this image of Jesus forward to me. I do know that since 2005, perhaps even earlier, Jesus has been trying to get my attention. I wanted to be a nun when I was a young teenager and wrote about some of my earlier encounters in my first book, entitled *A Soul's Journey*.

I don't think I put two and two together about my life, Jesus, and my abilities to talk to the other side until I was at church one day. As I was sitting in the pew listening to the minister, something dawned on me, a light went on, and it all began to make sense. That was a pivotal moment for me that would cause some positive shifting within my life. At that moment my gift made sense and my purpose had a new meaning. I finally felt normal and it even all happened in church!

When I began to feel more normal with my gift, I noticed something change in me. I felt a light grow within my soul. This light contained a pull and with it were thoughts I'd never had before, but they were positive thoughts. I began to feel at peace with these thoughts. I wanted the feeling to last. In fact, I loved the feeling and began to embrace it with all my heart and soul. It was the light that was awakening within my soul. However, each time I embraced this light, life tried to pull me back and fill me with fear, doubt, and pain. It is darkness that walks on this Earth and keeps many people from living a life full of truth and love. Yet, it's God's light that keeps reeling us back in. God is trying to show us a better way, but we live in conflict while trying to understand the truth. This is the truth of us and His truth for us. The conflict we engaged in leaves an opening in our soul that I call the rift, into which darkness can seep. Sometimes we need to surrender and have a little faith, so put your trust in God to keep the rift at bay.

When I finally opened my heart and my mind to the light that was waiting for me, I learned to shut out the negative pulls of life. I shut the door on darkness. When I closed the rift, I was able to enter the realm of true bliss, heaven on earth. When I stepped into this realm, after the door to darkness closed, I felt something, something different. It was a feeling I had never felt before. I don't have a word for this feeling because I've never experienced it before. And that's okay, as sometimes no words are needed, just an understanding. If I was to put a word to it, I'm pretty sure it was the Holy Spirit that I felt. The light I was experiencing was so overpowering, especially to a sensitive like me. As I became in balance with this source of energy, it felt like a new me had emerged through the darkness. It didn't happen overnight. It took many years of soul conflict for the light to integrate into the essence of who I am today. This light needed to transform me and my soul for it to awaken into its original form, which is love. This is all of our original energy pattern or soul form. We all have it in us if we choose the right path.

Every circumstance, each happy or painful event, is here to help you learn. Don't miss a thing in life. Keep your eyes open to the beauty that sits within you, listen to your soul, which is in the image of God. We're not alone here on Earth. Personally, I have a team of spiritual helpers on the other side. Some help me with my readings, while others help me with my personal and spiritual life, but two angels are always with me.

I have no doubt that living with one foot in heaven is going to change you. Once I began to listen to God and His angels, I started to take better care of myself. My own body is so sensitive because I am a medium. During the last eleven years my physical body has become even more responsive to the spirit world, making me more physically and spiritually sensitive. I struggled with this. What helped me? Well, besides prayer I discovered that Reiki healing was an integral healing modality that I needed to keep me balanced and grounded as a medium and as an empath. In fact I'm always doing self-healing on myself with Reiki. We all have a holy energy force around us. Reiki helped me to learn how to harness this, but we don't really need spiritual symbols or another kind of healing modality to help us. Rather, we need our hands, an ability to visualize, belief in prayer, a quiet mind, and an open heart. However, I've learned that Reiki symbols seem to enhance the healing process, which is interesting in itself. You have to experience it to truly understand my meaning regarding this. Even though I use my hands, the energy is coming from the Holy Spirit. I always start and end my session with a prayer and thanks to God. Reiki was an integral part of my healing many years ago and it still is today. At various times I teach it and offer Reiki healing to people who really need it. I believe the other side knew this was what I needed and that is how they got my attention, so I could move forward with my calling. The spirit world guided me to take Reiki, a powerful spiritual healing modality that I believe is a gift from God. Sometimes we just need labels to get us started on the path of realization and understanding. Hands-on healing and energy healing has been around since the beginning of time and is one of the oldest healing modalities. Today, many people see Reiki almost as something connected to the occult, but there's scientific proof that energy healing works and the spirit world has never said anything negative about it, not once. How could they, since energy healing is here to help people to heal.

As a medium, I've learned to have healthy boundaries with the world of spirit and this has helped me immensely. I can walk into a room without too much interference, go to the movies, hang out with friends, go to church, and the dead are not sitting around talking to me, thank goodness. I talk a lot about this because there is so much misinformation in our world regarding mediumship. It pains me when I see other mediums claiming they just can't shut it off, leaving others wondering and intrigued, thinking that every medium must be the same. Everyone's experiences are different and it's dangerous to be on or open all the time, feeling all the energy or souls around you. I don't care if most of this energy feels beautiful. It's not good for your soul. I don't believe good spirits are going to harass you, although evil spirits are a different story altogether. If you're being harassed from the average deceased, then you're not grounded with your calling and you haven't set proper boundaries.

CHAPTER TWO

~

The Reading

Most people consider the spirit world to be full of dead people, but I prefer saying the word deceased because, in reality, they are not dead. Death doesn't exist, whereas transformation does. Even though the physical body dies, the soul lives on. The body is simply the vessel for the soul, but many still prefer to use the word dead. And that's okay, since your loved ones don't mind and it's not disrespectful if you do call them dead. Whatever makes you feel comfortable is fine.

I've spoken to many deceased loved ones within the unseen realms and have the ability to connect with energy, so I seem to get a unique perspective regarding the person sitting in front of me. I can see their soul imprints and the strength and weakness within their soul. The pain I can see compels me to offer guidance, when this is needed. When you can help someone, and you know how to help them, you do what needs to be done. I feel it's about being in service. Soul imprints are messages and pain from the soul. Being able to read these imprints offers value to the client. These imprints bleed into the energy from the physical body, which is called the aura or energy field. Using my psychic empath abilities I can directly pick up the marks of the soul, as I'm reading spiritual energy. As a psychic empath I perceive the information that comes to me. However, my perceptions are always confirmed from my spiritual team on the other side. Believe me, they will tell me if I am wrong. This may be done in various ways, but when I am on the right track, I feel chills moving through my body. This is when I know to keep going, as the information coming through is correct. I'm being shown these soul imprints or marks as they need to be healed and heaven wants you to heal while you are on Earth. Soul imprints are also part of one's purpose, in the sense that the pain you went through in life is needed for your soul growth. When we heal from our past pains we can learn how to move forward or move on with life with the lesson already learned. This is where I come in during the reading. Based on specific symbols that were given to me, I see the purpose of the soul. For instance, I'll see a sign that tells me that a soul is a caregiver soul. Within this caregiver soul are many options one may take in their life. This is where free will comes in. A caregiver soul would make a good caregiver, a great counsellor, or a teacher. It really depends on what you as an individual desire to do and this could be based on your personality. You must stay within that purpose or your soul will feel unbalanced and a sense of emptiness may overcome you. Within the soul sit your future events. When I see these, I see a timeline, which could be within three months, six months, or within a year, maybe longer. You can never have an exact limit on your time as time is man-made. You can make things happen more quickly if you move through your life lessons at a faster pace. You can also stall your events altogether if you choose not to grow and move forward, this is the power within you. This is also why your loved ones have to be careful not to step on your timeline. You must grow on your own terms and even your angels will not interfere with your life lessons. This is why the death of a life is never given an exact time. You can postpone your death for a while, based on the choices you make today. That's comforting to know. And sometimes things are just meant to happen and this is the mystery of life.

My abilities also allow me to see colours within an aura, the energy field that floats around your physical body. The colours that are presented reveal the strength of your energy and physical body. We all have the colours of the rainbow around us and these colours will change in accordance with your emotional, physical, and mental state. On many occasions there will be a main colour that tells me the strength of your soul. It's interesting, since the strength of our soul always seems to be what we are fighting to move through. For example, I might see a blue colour that is associated with strong communication skills, yet the person I'm doing the reading for desires to have strong communication, so this is their fight or their life lesson on Earth. They're either scared to speak their truth or are learning how to be a better communicator, although some people have no problems at all. I might see a strong blue in a person's aura and intuitively know they are moving forward with their gift. Another colour may emerge that someone may need to work on or it may be a sign that an area of the soul needs to be healed. We're all unique and there's no firm requirement for the occurrence of these colours. Whether you surrender to your strengths or choose not to do so is a personal choice. The colours of our aura are parts of the soul and human body. Once you pass over into the afterlife, these colours leave you. They no longer remain with you in heaven, where they're not needed. You now have a new life on the other side.

I can comfortably say that the information I've learned to perceive is a psychic, intuitive knowing. The living spirit is talking to me and I know how to tune in, although I've never been taught this. However, I have done readings on the colours, even if I prefer to receive my guidance directly from spirit and my own soul. The information of the soul is identifying and I know it's meaning, yet I can't determine how I know this. The knowledge is extremely important to the success of the reading and the soul session. But remember, my spiritual team is never far away, as they watch over me. They will tell me if I'm wrong or try to get my attention in any way that they can.

Over the years I've learned that many sicknesses have a feeling. There's a symbol for specific mental health issues and our body speaks to us just like an illness does. It speaks to you and it speaks to me. However, for me to listen to the living spirit talk, I need to put my mind and body in a particular state of calmness. How do I do this? I put myself into prayer. Once this is done, I trust that the information I receive from the soul is the information my client needs in a reading. I'm very open to letting people know I don't believe in telling people their future and believe me our angels, deceased loved ones, and even the Holy Spirit would never provide information about finances or tell me something that would hinder my client's path. Can I see future events? Yes I can, but it all depends on what's to be revealed to my client and I have no control over what comes to me from my spiritual team on the other side. Knowledge of future events that come from the highest source of light is information that can help a person pull themselves toward the future. The information is provided to help you grow. The dead and the angels might inform one of an impending life change if it's imperative and the information is going to help you. However, they will not help you get any winning lottery numbers, tell you when your house is selling, interfere with other people's lives, or divulge information about another person that we would consider private, unnecessary or not for your highest good within a reading. It simply will not happen. Readings that inform our world or the family of missing persons or cold cases are very different from an individual reading that's simply offering guidance or speaking with a deceased loved one. Again, it's all about the intention. The reason you would like a reading always affects the outcome of the reading. The intention has to be used for good, not for evil. The other side doesn't like to waste time on ego driven desires.

I want to reaffirm that anyone seeing future events must come from a place that will help your life and guide you to make proper decisions and may even save your life. The topics discussed are always about your soul, health, healing, or your life. They act merely as a guide and don't tell you how to run your life or give you a definite answer regarding your health. With regards to health issues being mentioned in a reading, I believe that a collaboration of trained medical professions is required to provide you with a proper diagnosis. However, I can pick up early evidence of illness before this is measured or detected through the medical system. It's happened many, many times before. I don't advertise that I'm able to this, as it's not good spiritual practice. Too many unrealistic expectations can emerge from giving such advice and I trust spirit will deliver what needs to be delivered. I don't try to put myself on a pedestal of knowledge. This is not in alignment with heaven's motives of sacred information.

I find my sessions are more powerful and soul changing when a person is guided toward positive change and learns how to experience life differently, allowing them to feel and experience their accomplishments on their terms. Knowing and feeling they did the work for their achievements can be life changing and is vital for soul growth.

As a medium that receives information from the deceased, I want to explain what I've been told directly from the other side and have experienced myself. Your deceased loved ones want to talk to you, but they don't wish to be responsible for the decisions you make. They will help you to a certain extent, but don't want you to rely on them. I get it. We do have to find our own way in the world, but the information they share can be positively life changing. And if you have questions about them and their life that you need to clarify, they will tell you what they need you to do.

Why are they so careful in a reading? Life changes, just like waves change direction when needed. The current controls the waves, even though you are the one steering your boat. The best way to approach a reading is to let it unfold. Trust that your deceased loved ones, God, and His angels know what you need. And never ask questions that would be prying into one's life. This is a big no-no on the other side. Some questions that are considered to be prying. Is my husband cheating? Is my spouse going to get a raise? Is my daughter taking drugs or seeing someone? What's happening with my sister's or brother's kids? Does my boss have a mental illness? We might get information about the mental health of close families, but only if this is important for one to know. We will not obtain health information

11

related to people outside our family dynamic. This is none of our business and spirit won't answer during readings. A medium or a psychic can gather all kinds of information about the dead, primarily because the dead are telling us. If they want to divulge information about themselves and their mental health when they were alive, then all is good.

I remember in one of my spiritual psychic readings, which is what I use to call them, a woman demanded that I tell her who her husband was having an affair with, placing three photos on the table. I quickly replied that I had no idea and didn't do those kinds of readings. God and the afterlife, don't like these questions and I don't ask them of my team on the other side. I believe that people ask such questions because they are in pain or desperately need resolution. I think some people have the wrong impression or information about mediums and psychics. In my opinion, people either feel they have the right to know or that it's okay to ask these kinds of questions when they are paying for the service. This can put the medium in a bad predicament, as the client takes control of the reading when they have no real idea what they're asking or drawing close to them with these kinds of questions. In reality, I think the client feels they have more power within the reading than the psychic, medium, or even their deceased loved one. This is simply because our world is conditioned to think this way. Readings like this aren't in alignment with heaven, they are ego driven, and I personally won't even entertain them. This is the easiest way to draw in negative energy as you are not in a divine flow, which means your energy vibration is low and you can attract lower energies. This doesn't occur during the reading, but afterward. Sound confusing? There's more to readings and the afterlife than one may think. I take pride knowing I live within certain ethics parameters and requirements when engaged in readings. Every medium should adhere to a code of ethics, in order to help their clients within their lives and honour their gift and the world of spirit, but many mediums don't do this.

As for privacy regarding other people's lives, I'm a firm believer in personal privacy and the spirit world knows this. They would never make me tell a stranger that their dead aunt would like to give them a message. This isn't going to happen with my life, not when I haven't set the intention to let spirit speak with me. I get a lot of questions like this, wondering if the dead are always talking to me. Yet it's important to remember that when I do house or location walkthroughs or carry out a group reading, I've set the intention for spirit to communicate with me, as I'm working. Life is all about your intention. This is when the deceased and the angels know I'm open to receive their information. When I'm not working, they are careful and don't bother me too much. However, they can deliver a message through my feelings and I may be compelled to say something that helps another person, without knowing that this information is coming directly from the deceased or even from an angel. The dead have learned a great deal from being in heaven. They are sincere, patient, positive, and full of wisdom.

One day I was at a birthday party and an older man came over and started talking. I knew a little about him and I began to ask some questions about his farm without knowing why, since I am by no means a farmer. He started to talk about it and I began speaking about changes in farming and how he should look at other options for growing vegetables. Then before I could stop myself, I said that the farm had been in his family for decades, his dad was proud of him and what he'd done and that he'd exceeded his expectations. The man smiled and said that he'd never thought of it that way, but hope that what I said was true. I then informed him that whatever he decided to do with the farm, his dad was okay with it. After the conversation finished, I realized that the man's deceased father had been talking to me and respectfully giving me information without intruding into my space or that of his son. Sometimes I get information to help another soul and I have no idea who's talking. Now that's love and respect from spirit.

This kind of spirit communication is good and it felt as if it was being directed from the light. However, I didn't say that I thought his dad was there and had some information to share. What if the person didn't believe in life after death and ignored the message if I stated where it came from? God uses us when He needs us and the dead will speak to us when they need to. You just need to watch for the message. Remember, as a medium I'm a receiver of deceased and divine information.

Because of this, I don't believe in using any form of divination tool to get information from God, angels, or your deceased loved ones. It's simply not a good spiritual practice to have. Instead, spirit wants you to be more aware of your intuitive gift and the messages that come for you from spirit. You can do this with prayer. God and the light cannot enter into objects, but the dark can. This is because of the intention. If we're asking questions based on fear, ego desires, for fun, or with negative intention, this seems to open doors one should not open. By doing this, you're giving dark energy permission to enter your life.

This is why I only use prayer, which brings forward the light. The light carries free will and the desire for one to experience the power that resides within them and the need to believe and have faith that God is with them. Silencing the mind, engaging in prayer, and learning how to listen to the voice of God will help you more than any divination tool, such as tarot cards, the pendulum, ruins, stones, crystal ball gazing, or spirit boards. A medium needs nothing to connect with the other side, only to have faith in God and a strong belief that life goes on, even after death.

When your soul is so close in another realm, it's inevitable that you're going to have experience with the light and the dark. This is what can be scary at times for many people. I'm sure you have heard the phrase that your experiences are coming from your thoughts. While this is often true, we experience what we need for our soul to grow and this is not coming from your mind. It's arising from your soul lessons or the contract you have with your soul. Your soul lesson is very different from your daily actions or your reactions to the thoughts you're attracting in your life. Many people get confused about this. You don't draw everything into your experience based on your thoughts and I don't believe in karma.

Karma says what you put out into the universe comes back to

you. This means that if you do something negative or harmful to someone, you will get that back. While this sounds good, I don't believe in it anymore. It tells us destiny isn't real and God is already judging before one has time to change and repent of one's sins. How can you say karma is real when someone's gone through huge losses in their life and every time they turn around something goes wrong. I've seen a lot of evil people in my life and so far all is good for them. Can we say people deserve what they get or you did something terrible to someone at some point on your soul journey, so you need to experience pain? Or that good comes to you because you do good things? The most bizarre phrase I've heard states that if someone did something bad to you, you must have done something bad to someone else. Really? I don't think so. I've asked the afterlife, my angels, and been told that the answer is no. You can be assured that God and the angels see everything and retribution seems to happen after one dies. Now that doesn't mean there isn't the law of cause and effect, because there is.

If you do something wrong in our physical world, you're punished by something such as jail time. But our life lives on after death. I've had a lot of terrible experiences in my life. I've met many people that I would consider evil and I'm in no way, shape, or form a mean or evil person. It seems when people see evil people getting away with things, they immediately turn to God and ask why He allows it. Or they might claim that this is proof that there's no God, since no true version of God would allow such things to happen. This type of thinking or truth is going to turn you away from Him. Our human world is ours. It was a gift from the Creator. Even though God is present, He also lets us live our lives, fall, or make mistakes so we can learn and when we learn, we can become closer to Him. I can guarantee you God doesn't pick favourites and if you've heard this claim from someone, it's only their ego calling the shots, not God. Can we honestly say God should run around damming everyone that has done something wrong in the human world? He might be omnipresent, but I don't think this is His job. God controls the afterlife, but we seem to control the physical world, or at least some of it.

People often ask me if I can shut it off my experiences from the afterlife. The answer is yes, and no. The dead are always around. I learned when I was eleven that I could silence the spirit voices only for a short time. This is when I learned how to create firm boundaries with spirit. I'd sometimes walk to school with friends and sometimes I'd walk alone. When I was alone, I always heard little words and on many occasions a female voice calling my name. Without really knowing what was going on, I asked out loud if whatever or whomever it was could please stop talking to me. They did until I was about fourteen or fifteen, when it came back tenfold. You see, when I was a child, I asked some of my friends if they heard people talking or saw people that weren't there. Let us say that I got a lot of strange looks! But that was in the seventies. These days, I can shut it off for a while, but I can't just wake up and say that I don't want to be a medium or see or talk to the dead. It doesn't work that way, not when you are born with the gift and really are talking to deceased loved ones in heaven. I was born a sensitive and I was born an empath too. I must use my gifts for good. This is why I call it a gift. I can turn the dial down when I need to live my life. I was born with some kind of an opening within my soul that allows me to communicate with the unseen worlds. I close this opening when I prefer not to receive spirit information. When I'm ready to receive I open it. This opening can't be closed permanently. If I try to do that I became imbalanced within my own energy field, leaving me feeling not so good. This is why it's a gift. I receive information to give information.

It's tough not to be bothered by what some people may think of me and what I do. I've heard people say that talking to the dead is the work of evil. While I do believe evil is real, I'm not talking to demons. I'm talking to a person's loved ones when I do readings. I'll explore evil and negative energy later. I'd lost many friends when I began this work, yet also lost many friends when I expressed my belief in Jesus. You can't please everyone and I don't think this is something we should even strive for.

What keeps me strong or unconcerned about what other people think? I keep remembering all the thousands of people I've helped and all the strong validation and evidence I've been able to bring forward for my clients, information I would never or could never have known in any other way. And when I see the peace and healing that enters into other lives as a result of what I do, everything I've had to go through to get where I am today was well worth the fight. Looking positively at life lessons is something we all need to have within our lives, especially when we live in a world that's always trying to knock us down. Sometimes people don't like happy individuals. It was a lesson I needed to learn. Prayer is also one of the best ways to keep your energy vibration on track. In fact, when I'm feeling a little unbalanced within my energy field, I often put both hands over top of my heart, one under the other, and say these simple words as a reminder to my soul and to the consciousness.

"I am at peace, my life is at peace, and I am where I need to be at this moment in time."

Now if I want to take it one step further, which I often do, I say something else at the end.

"In God I trust."

This helps me stay positive and it can help you too. Give it a try.

It's important to remember that we're all surrounded by love. Nothing that comes from the heavenly realms can harm you. Harm can only come from the lower levels within the spirit realms, and only if you permit it to do so. Evil needs your direct permission for it to enter into your world. Negative spirit experiences can hurt your soul and some never recover from this. That's why I incorporate Jesus and the Holy Spirit into every reading. Not everyone knows I'm doing this, but I do and that's important to me. I don't believe that Jesus or the Holy Spirit is telling me everything. This spiritual force of love is merely protecting me. I started to do readings back in 2008 and one or two years later a woman came to see me. I could sense something was not right and that she wasn't authentic. You know that feeling you have when someone says something but you feel they have ulterior motives? This is called reading between the lines, with love. She also asked questions during the reading that she shouldn't have been asking, but I didn't know any better at the time. She enjoyed the reading and as she opened the door to leave, she turned and looked straight into my eyes and told me that I was gifted and had a good thing going. I thanked her then she added that I shouldn't screw it up and keep God out of it. I was shocked and even today I often wonder what was around her, which was obviously not God. This was painful. Can we honestly say there's not one being governing this world? It doesn't make sense to me. Since I'm a receiver of information from the deceased I must conduct my life in the way that I've been shown from heaven. This is good spiritual practice. At the beginning of the book I mentioned that God might be another word for you and that this is okay. To believe that nothing is governing our world, or that there's no meaning to us or to our life, is not okay. I don't think our brain or soul is hardwired this way. If we don't believe in anything, I believe that our soul is already dying.

Miracles happen all the time, people heal and people change. One has to open their hearts and mind for positive change to occur. While this may sound easy, it isn't, but it's a choice and a decision one may make. My life isn't regular or even average and I never pretend it is, not anymore. The people who come to see me need peace. They need to speak with their loved ones once more. They need to know there's more to this living life. I often deliver messages from souls that passed from suicide and their loved ones need to know why. Sometimes there are murders and unusual deaths and we need to understand how and why these happened.

I remember one woman that came for a reading. When the medium reading started, I could feel all her pain, depression, and desire to die. Our body talks to us if we allow it. I've worked with many clients who have similar feelings until they have a reading. My client had recently lost a husband to a sudden heart attack, a child to a drug overdose, and her mother to cancer, all within one year. How does a person go on? She was devastated and wanted to die. I was worried about her and after the reading, we talked. She said she didn't want to go on anymore and wanted to be with her loved ones in heaven. I asked some critical questions and then told her about the other side, which I'll further discuss later.

"If you take your own life before your time, there's no guarantee you will spend much time with your loved ones," I explained. "Over the years the dead have told me that if you take your own life, you see your loved ones briefly, but you go into a soul healing and when this happens, you're not with your loved ones."

You see, there's no time in the spirit world and there doesn't need to be any. Consequently, we don't know if one day is a month or a month feels like one day, since this is all determined by the higher powers in the higher realms. By being truthful and telling her what I had seen, she changed her mind. I told her the best thing you can do for your loved ones in heaven is to heal. When you heal, they heal. Imagine seeing your loved ones in pain and you can't do anything about it. I genuinely believe that's why so many of my clients were told by their loved ones in their dreams to see me or they found me in interesting ways. The dead need a voice and that's what I provide. My client left the reading with a sense of peace and healing. She was ready to move on with the life God had given her to live. Would my client have received so much peace if she hadn't had a reading? Or would she have chosen the wrong way out?

Grief and losing a loved one is painful. There's no time frame for grief, as everyone is different and everyone grieves in their own way. With the pain of grief, you need to take one day at a time and one step at a time toward healing for complete wholeness to take place, whatever that may mean to you.

Readings can be exhausting sometimes, but I've learned to live with it and release the energies as soon as I finish my sessions. I hold on to nothing. I've also learned to identify my pain and the pain of the afterlife. It took some time to learn how to do this, but I figured out a way. When I see healing take place like it did in my client's case, it makes my love for my purpose even more satisfying. I love it when I can help the living and the deceased souls to heal by just being a voice for them both. One woman was very honest with me after we finished her reading.

"Marnie, I want to thank you for all the readings you've done," she said. "You may not know this, but I wanted to die and your readings have given me the will to live. You seriously saved my life. You've helped me more than anyone else could ever have and I'm so grateful for what you do."

When you see this kind of healing take place, it feels like God has played a major role in the process.

Even though readings can be exhausting, my gift fulfills my soul and I am grateful it helps so many people. I support the dead and heal the living with what I do. I believe all mediums receive information unique to their abilities. For myself, I am a physical and a mental medium. I use clairvoyance, also known as clear seeing. Can I see spirit? Yes, I can see how they look in my mind and I have seen them in the physical world too. Sometimes I see images of white ghostly figures moving around and I have seen dark ghostly figures, which I call dark souls. Using claircognizance the spirit world puts impressions into my mind and provides me with precise knowledge. The information I see, hear, and feel from the spirit world is sent to me where I will understand what they are trying to convey. I see symbols which are unique to my understanding. I can hear the voice of spirit within my mind and outside of myself, through my ears, this is called clairaudience. When I feel the spirit world, I sometimes I get chills or feel warm when this happens. Using clairsentience, I feel how the dead have passed. I may get chest pains, which indicates heart issues, or my breathing may become difficult, which means they had a chest or lung issue and couldn't breathe near the end of their life. I can feel their emotions when they were alive, this is called clairempathy. And it's not unusual to smell certain perfumes or flowers that they loved; this is clairsalinece. While it is rare, I can taste what I need to taste from the world of spirit, also known as clairgustance. If I need to get information from something that belonged to the decease I can touch objects and get specific information, this is also called psychometry or clairtangency. While it's never needed in my readings, it can be used in missing persons or cold cases. The way I see it, the reading always turns out the way you need to receive it. All to help you heal.

CHAPTER THREE

~

Spirit Visitations

I've had missing people show up while I was alone, telling me things about themselves, and I've experienced spirits arriving at night and talking to me too. This doesn't seem even to faze me anymore. One night I woke up and a man was standing beside my bed, close to the window. He was wearing indigenous clothing. I asked him what he wanted and he replied that he was just passing through, saw my light, and wanted to say hello. My bedroom light wasn't on. It was my aura that he was picking up. The deceased do know how to find the people that can communicate with them. In the morning, I was reminded that there's a reserve located close to my home. Perhaps the man was coming from one of his visits there.

Sometimes spirit communication can be a little nerve-wracking too. Earlier in my career, a woman showed up at night. The evenings are always more accessible for the spirit world to communicate. This has a lot to do with the energy vibration of our planet, so there's less interference for communication. She pleaded with me, needing me to help her daughter, yet she never gave me a name. I explained that I didn't know who her daughter was and that she should ask her to call me. I have had many people tell me their parents visit them in

21

their dreams and tell them things. I have no control over when they show up like this and they know they aren't invited to show up when I'm with my children.

Okay, so we're going to talk a little about how negative energy or evil can affect me. I know this kind of thing is scary, but it's real. I'll talk more about it later, but evil is also part of the spirit realm. Not only can I see darkness, I can smell it too and it isn't fun. Oh, I've seen some scary attachments on people, believe me. I've also seen them leave their souls and make room for the light to enter. That's a beautiful sight. These are some of the things that I experienced daily. When I talk to happy people, people who are excited to talk to their loved ones, and it's reciprocated on the other side, my energy level is high. However, it can lessen when I speak with deceased individuals that have committed suicide. Even though everyone goes to the other side, there are different levels within heaven too. The lower level is very, very real, and I don't call it heaven and neither does the spirit world. Every soul needs to learn how they could have done things better when they were in our world.

Our world is our classroom and the learning doesn't stop when you reach heaven, it continues. It's essential to heal your soul, today, in the physical world and learn how to allow God to enter into your life. When evil or negative energy is nearby, I feel dizzy and sick to my stomach. I've learned how to protect myself whenever I get into those situations. Usually, this happens when I do house blessing and clearings or during home or location spirit investigations. While I experience other people's negative energy during a reading, an evil spirit or demon has never come through and talked with me during a private or a group session. It simply doesn't happen. My intention is about healing, bringing forward validation and healing to my client, and this usually comes from loved ones.

If I know there's an attachment, I start teaching the people how to deal with it so it will disappear from their lives. There are certain things you can do while not divulging to the spirit world exactly what you're doing. Eventually, negative energy will get bored if it's not fed and will leave the soul. I remember when I first told someone, a former friend, that I could see evil. They said that this wasn't right and that there must be something wrong with me. I no longer tell people half the stuff I know and have seen. It might feel like a horror book if I did. I've learned to be okay with it because this is called spiritual discernment, an ability that can't be completely understood since it's associated with being me. As I stated earlier, spiritual insight involves being able to identify good and evil spirits. If it's going to help another soul heal on this planet and bring awareness into the world regarding good and evil, then I need to experience it. It's also a part of my journey and if you think talking with the deceased was hard for me to swallow, imagine how I felt when I first realized that I could see evil.

On many occasions, before a reading, I'll have a loved one come in and say hello. They tell me who they are and are eager and happy to talk to their loved ones. I often have them saying thank you as well. The conversation is usually very brief. They know when they can speak to me and when they can't. My door to heaven opens up in the morning on the days when I'm working then closes at the end of my reading day.

It isn't unusual for me to become hot when there's a lot of spirit energy around. At that point I know I need to go or I might start to feel shaky or take on either their illness or feel those of the spirits. That's my empathic ability. I don't like visiting hospitals. On two different occasions, I heard the deceased speak with me at a hospital and trust me, they were scary situations. Once I was getting ready for surgery and as I was laying down I heard a male voice, say that it was a good day to die.

"No," I said. "It isn't. In the power of Jesus Christ, I command you to leave now."

He did and I survived. The second incident happened when I was recovering from another surgery and began to hear and see deceased people that didn't want to cross over as they were afraid to go to the light. So I was lying in bed in my hospital room, trying to cross souls over and tell them not to be afraid and go to the light, all while I was trying to rest. Why were these souls interacting with me?

Well, they didn't know any better. They hadn't seen the other side and were afraid to go either with their loved ones or with the angels that were trying to escort them into heaven. The deceased knew that I could help them and they were desperate. They finally left me and I guess it was my calming voice that persuaded them because they did stop bothering me. At that time I was in no shape to argue with any spirit about when they could or couldn't speak with me. Sometimes you need to pick your battles and surrender when needed.

It's not unusual for me to help souls cross over and this is when messages have been brought forward to their loved ones. They know how to walk to the light, but sometimes they're afraid. I did a reading for a young woman that had lost her mother to suicide. She felt her mother's presence around her and wanted to find out what she had to say. I delivered the messages and the deceased seemed to be good, but I could feel a sense of restlessness with the mother. About a month later I got a call and the young woman said that her mother was around in the house and this was making her feel uneasy. I went to do a house clearing and blessing and believe me her mother wasn't the only spirit hanging around. I completed the house clearing and blessing and crossed her mother over, reassuring her that everyone was at peace and ready for her to move forward to the other side. She had more to say, which was why she didn't seem to feel at peace, but once the message was delivered, there were no more unusual or unexplained experiences. Sometimes my work is never done.

Spirit is everywhere. It's interesting how many lights I seem to see within the room when I'm sitting in my bed reading in the evening or even when talking to people. The sparkles I see are like stars glittering around someone or on the wall. This light may be either your loved one saying hello or an angel reminding you that you are loved. I always thank them, but never ask for more. It's nice to know that no one is truly alone. You may wonder why you haven't seen any stars or flickering lights? Not to worry, this is usually caused by your left braining closing the images off due to fear. Our mind wants to protect us and if something seems a little strange, we may not see it. However, if you see lights frequently and they are large, make sure you get your eyes checked and that you see your doctor. Not everything that happens in our life is related to spirit communication.

One day my husband and I were on holidays and I was visiting a family home. It was just the four of us, my husband and two children. When I walked in the front door, I could feel my deceased grandma and grandpa, but not my father or anyone else, and that was okay. The children were downstairs and my husband and I were sitting at the kitchen table. I looked at him and suddenly saw a massive light to the left of him and to my right. He asked if I was okay, but I couldn't answer right away. I then explained that there was this big light that kept getting bigger. I told him that his grandma was coming through and my husband asked if she was saying anything.

"She's waving, saying hello," I replied. "She's beautiful and wants you to know she's watching over you."

She really did look beautiful. I mean this lady had the most delicate skin I'd ever seen when she was alive. She presented herself first as I remembered her and then she began to look younger. Before I could say anything, my husband looked at me and was in shock.

"Marnie," he said. "Last night I was wondering why my grandmother has never visited you or why she's never shown herself. I thought maybe she wasn't with me."

Well, that morning around 10:00 am while having a cup of coffee, my husband received his answer. Yes, she heard him. He never said this out loud but rather she listened to his thoughts. God hears us and so do our loved ones in heaven. However, I must stress that just because they can listen to us doesn't mean they can help us. That's just the way it works.

It took me years to understand that being sensitive isn't connected with any New Age, spiritualist or metaphysical movement, but is something that has been around since the beginning of time. God knows what He's doing. If you're a sensitive or an empath you don't have to enter into some spiritualist area. Accept you for who you are and move on. In time you'll understand why God gave you the gift.

It's not an easy journey, but you can do it. My empathic abilities are here to help me with my readings.

I remember one day doing a reading for a woman just after I'd finished another one. I'd completed a reading for a mother whose son had committed suicide, so my energy level was a little low and my throat hurt from the previous session. Her son had hung himself and as soon as I made the connection, I told her that her son was with us and that he'd died from suicide. When I then felt like I was choking, I said that her son had hung himself, which she confirmed. My throat felt a little sore and it was a very emotional reading. During my next reading right afterward, I had to take care of myself and heaven knew this. When I entered into the reading, I had a kind gentleman came forward that was the father of my client.

"Your father is here and he's such a kind soul," I said.

He then simply told me that my body was tired and that I should just tell her that he'd died from a heart attack and that I didn't need to feel that pain.

I told my client that her dad had passed away from a heart attack, which she verified. I also told her why he'd said it this way.

I have learned that there is a higher power watching out for me during my readings and making sure my body or my mind is not being too affected. It's a nice feeling as a sensitive, empathic, and physical medium. The best way I can explain this type of mediumship is that it feels like the deceased soul merges with my soul and I can feel all their feelings and memories. Sometimes it feels like they're providing me with images and painting me a picture of their life. I can feel how they passed, their previous illness including physical and mental health issues, and can feel their pain and their happiness. However, if the soul isn't on the right level within heaven, let's say they weren't a kind soul in the physical world, a barrier of energy appears and I can't feel anything from them. Their soul is in healing and cannot merge with mine, so mental mediumship begins. With mental mediumship, I get impressions of their life, with no feelings at all. I'll hear them and even smell certain things, but the reading is undertaken with caution. I usually inform my clients regarding what level they are on. It can be hard to hear that your loved one needs a tremendous amount of healing on the other side, but this is always confirmed and verified as authentic.

This spirit world is very open to providing us with information that's meant to help us. Sometimes you need to ask them and I do this frequently. I ask the deceased if there's anything that they would like to tell me about heaven or their experiences so far? The dead are always very open with me. In a reading, I just let them speak, but I test them first. There are some things they have to tell me, such as how they passed, although I usually feel this, how they're connected to my client, what side of the family they're from and then they need to give me some other form of information about themselves. Sometimes this is their name, initials, the dates of their passing or upcoming birthdays and so on then I just let them say what they want to tell me. There's no pressure on either side and I stress in my readings that you should never demand anything from your loved one. I can't tell you how many times people have told others to ask a loved one to bring through their favourite colour or their favourite food or something only the client and the dead would know. On many occasions, this comes through naturally, but what if I was unable to understand your loved one? Maybe the colours were off that day or perhaps I couldn't hear and only see on that day. Always let the reading unfold as it needs to.

When I meet people for the first time, I'm always asked what I do. I feel the person out and if I'm unsure of their reaction I usually take the safe route or answer the question with least resistance on their part by saying that I work as a grief coach. I was once introduced to a man that my husband also knew as an acquaintance and was asked this question. I felt a strong pull to tell this man the truth, so when introductions came and he asked me what I did for a living I replied that I was a medium. He asked if this meant that I talked to dead people, which I confirmed. I then paused for a moment, waiting for some reaction. However, I received the most crucial question, one I was thrilled to answer.

"Can I ask you a question, a personal question?" he said.

I agreed and he told me I could tell him where to go if I didn't want to answer the question. I giggled and became even more intrigued.

"Do you believe in the Messiah?" he asked.

"You mean Jesus Christ?" I replied.

"Yes," he said.

"Absolutely," I replied. "There's no doubt in my mind that Jesus was divine and is still very much alive in spirit."

I also told him how I believed in heaven and that we do go somewhere when we pass. He thanked me for my answer and looked at my husband and I.

"Who better to ask this question," he said. "You have no reason to tell me anything different from what you believe and have experienced."

Now here's a more negative example regarding a communicative experience as a medium, or people asking me what I do. I was taking a weekend workshop that didn't involve any spiritual stuff, so decided to keep a low profile. On the last day, I was having lunch and two women asked if they could sit at my table. I said that it was fine and as soon as the conversation began the question of the hour was what do I do? I was very honest about what I did and one of the women almost fell off her chair. She seemed nice at first, but I could see her demeanour change within seconds. That kind soul turned sour and she expressed her opinions, so at the end I simply stated that we all see things differently. Today, I don't take the path of least resistance. In fact, I'm pleased to be a medium and when asked what I do for a living I look people in the eye with a bright smile and say I'm a medium and that I help the living world and the dead heal.

My devotion to God and being a truth seeker is what truly guides me on my path. I believe the spirit communication between heaven and Earth is a holy one and feel that the other side has entrusted me to be one of their messenger of truth, love, and light. I know that there's a higher power and a force of light governing my work as a medium. I'll always do my best and do the work they have entrusted me with. I know what waits for me on the other side.

One day a woman came to visit me and I knew her but not really well. She told me how her back hurt and since I didn't know anything about her health, I automatically looked within her body and could see that bones seemed to be misaligned in her back. There was nerve pain and I could feel it. The following week I spoke with her.

"Marnie, my back is feeling better," she explained. "Between you and my doctor I'm hoping my back will stay this way."

I was a little confused, so she clarified what she meant.

"Well, I didn't want to mention anything when we were talking before, but your eyes changed that night, just before you gave me your suggestions. My husband was with me, along with her husband, and I asked her if they'd turned white or anything like that and we all laughed.

"Your eyes didn't change colour, but your pupils got big," she said. "I can't explain it, but I know you were sending me some form of healing. I felt something, I felt different, at peace, so thank you for whatever you did."

A little shocked to hear this woman speaking of this, I simply told her that I was so glad that my presence had made a difference. You see, when she was talking with me about her pain, spirit was already working through me. The spirit world knew what she needed and as a medium I'm a conduit for a divine energy force. I then proceeded to tell them about a group reading when a woman told me that the whole time I was talking to deceased loved ones, I had a beautiful glowing white light all around me that covered my entire body. She couldn't believe it, it was so beautiful.

This woman could see spirit energy.

When I listened to the woman that was visiting tell me her story, I remembered that without hesitation I had automatically scanned her body. I saw the pain and I sent love to it.

"Jesus, Lord," I said. "Please give her your light of love and healing to the areas in her body that need your blessings and healing, thank you."

This was an automatic response to her pain. Was any of this a coincidence? I believe coincidences are God's way of being anonymous.

The spirit world uses my gift when needed and remember, they're always present and I'm a Reiki Master.

I was born with my gift and never pursued it, but did have to choose to accept it. I've struggled dearly with my choices and somehow still struggle with it today. My faith falls under Christianity and that doesn't make a lot of sense to people. Some people have asked me how can you do what you do when you believe in what you believe. Well, I say it isn't easy, but I believe what I can see, what I know, and what I feel, not what someone tells me to think. By following the guidance from the Holy Spirit, I now understand how I can help people with what I do. I've learned over the years that Jesus pursues us with love and his messages are about love and healing. If we listen and open our hearts and mind, He will talk to us and show us the way. And I know deep within my soul that I don't think speaking to the deceased is evil if done in the proper way. To get through, I remind myself that Jesus isn't about religion. He is about love, respect, kindness, truth, and positive teachings and I need Him to be in my life with what I do. It's interesting since when I was on my faith journey and trying to make sense of my gift I had a strong understanding come forward to me, during Pentecost. Yes, the Holy Spirit works in mysterious ways. This is why my journey to surrender to Jesus was important.

During a reading, you can feel when God and His angels are present and the information is coming from a higher source. The information is about love, forgiveness, moving forward, and learning how to live your best life, not necessarily just for you, but for everyone. God is about the word 'we' not just the word 'me'.

CHAPTER FOUR

~

When Jesus Showed Up And Why

God's intention for us is to learn how we can all get along, as a family. My relationship with Jesus is a very personal one and I think this is also true for many people. After reading this, perhaps you will understand why I speak of Jesus so much. Over the years, I have been very open about my faith and my belief in Jesus Christ and not everyone is comfortable with this. However, my religion is love and in case anyone is wondering, I'm following and experiencing the real Jesus Christ. There seems to be some discrepancy with this. I've heard on many occasions from various spiritual leaders that if you're a medium and Jesus comes to you or is speaking to you and wants you to continue talking to the dead, then it must be the false Christ. I don't believe this at all. Jesus is in the spiritual realms and He is for everyone who wants to follow Him. After all, He is a spirit now, as He once had a human form. Jesus is for everyone and all you have to do is let him into your world. It pains me when I see what we've done negatively as a society with His name. I won't get into the mechanics of the Bible at this time and I certainly don't disagree with everything that's contained in the Bible.

Over the years, the closer I got to Jesus, I noticed something was happening to me. I could feel it, it was good, so I went with it. It was the Holy Spirit, again. God sends this source of energy to all who need it and are willing to accept it. God was speaking to me through my intuition and He was working at changing me, guiding me on my path. Even though I give messages and evidence to the living as a medium, messages that are directed to me from spirit come through differently. I think this is true for all of us.

I have an authoritative demeanour and have heard spirit voices for so long that I sometimes ignore messages that are coming to me personally. It's a nasty habit I got myself into but I'm learning to listen. I think this is an automatic response, something I learned long ago. I learned to not listen to spiritual guidance because of fear. It had a lot to do with getting into a habit of shutting the spirit world out, so I wouldn't feel weird or have people think I was crazy. However, the spirit world knows this, so they keep pursuing. God has an image for all of us. In essence, I believe we're here to be like Jesus, to love, help, guide, and to be in service to God.

There are teachings in the Old Testament and in the New Testament and I feel every word written within the Bible is open to interpretation. This is no different to what everything one says, sees, hears, or reads also being open to individual analysis. God knows how to find His people and how to bring them closer to Him. Perhaps we need to trust Him more. Yet he needs us to do His work. This has been a difficult task for many, to trust what we cannot see, especially a God that many fear. Our brain is hard wired for fear. Ancestrally we needed this fear, if we were to survive in life in ancient times. However, we don't need to be in fear so much anymore. Life is different now but as humans many continue to live with the fight. I've often thought if people even know anymore why they're fighting, why they continue to go down the path of fear and negativity. Bad habits are hard to break and if one doesn't know any better they continue going the same way that they always have. We gravitate toward what is familiar to us.

Jesus understood that fighting with the dark can only be done with light or love. I feel this is why He spent time around the unfortunate, the ones who were criminals, people with hate and anger, those that were left behind, the ones that were ignored and persecuted for their ways or their sickness. He knew people could change for the better when they felt cared for and loved. His actions attempted to show us how we all need to be, more accepting and more loving of God's creations.

Within this book, I'm only sharing my personal experiences. I understand what sits within my heart and what I've learned and experienced throughout my life so far. I believe we are of love, we will return to love, and we're here to understand and embrace love. We're here to be in service as a 'we' society not a 'me' society. And if it's God's will, we will struggle.

One of the scariest moments in my life regarding Jesus was while I was writing this book. I went for coffee with a good friend.

"You know as I write this book, I think I'm going to have to make a choice about my faith," I said.

She asked me what I meant and I explained that from what I'd been reading, learning, and experiencing, I might have to choose my faith over being a medium. I believed that I needed to choose, remain a Christian or say goodbye to Jesus and continue being a medium. I was feeling as if I couldn't possible do both. Well, my friend's eyes widened and I know even saying these words felt wrong, since she was shaking her head in disbelief. Then I thought about it a little more deeply.

"Why am I allowing so much conflict within my life based on what other people are saying and doing about Jesus?" I said.

Leaving Jesus felt wrong. It felt lonely and I felt empty at the mere thought of doing such a thing. The thought was just as painful as losing a loved one through death. I knew that if I left Him, my life would never be the same and I didn't want to leave Him, not then, not now, not ever. On some level, I felt religion was making me arrive at a decision or was it society that was doing that? Either way, it was a decision I didn't feel comfortable making. Yet I knew that I needed to make a decision. I was helping so many people with what I could do. Jesus reassured me that I should follow Him and trust Him on my path. I was being asked to trust Him and love what He brought into my life. I was to have faith that understanding would come in time, directly from Him. Most of all I was to ignore what the human world was trying to tell me that was causing so much negativity and pain within my life. It was causing me too much unneeded conflict within my soul. The dead and the living needed my voice, end of story.

I decided to step out into my life, embrace who I am and all its uniqueness and just be me. And I work hard every day to make sure societal fears do not disturb my life too much and ignore what people say about me being a medium. Putting people down for their natural born gifts? You can tell when Jesus has his hands in something and when the devil does too, if you look closely. Our world seems so distorted by labels that ancient words or modern day ones alter thoughts. Words have power, but powerful words need direction to positive thoughts and that isn't always to the case with our world. We lift people and bring them closer to God by showing them love. Not by judging them, but by loving them and by getting out of God's way. Let God work the miracles for each person's life. It's no wonder that we don't see many miracles any more. We judge too much instead of trying to show others sincere understanding, genuine friendship, and love. Choose to be the ear that listens without judgement. Who are we to judge anyway? Jesus came to start a community, a community of faith and love, not a world of religion. A religion that causes hate and disruption is totally opposed to why Jesus was born and resurrected. God wants His family to get along so we must pave the path in His name. Pave that path so perfectly and so full of light and love that it can shine to the heavens above and into the darkest places so that all people would desire to walk on it.

When Jesus entered my life, I became even happier. I feel safe. I feel at rest and cared for. It's important in life to remember that the dark holds no power. Eventually, the light comes in and washes it all away, but only if you let it in. You can't have both Satan and Jesus within your life at the same time. It doesn't work.

Sometimes we need help to get the dark removed and Satan isn't able to hide for long. I'm sure he gets bored masquerading around like an angel of light. He wants power and he wants disturbance. He moves toward the real power that's in our world. But be forewarned, he doesn't work alone and he would love to get his hands and pointy fingernails on any soul that delves into the light. The devil wants to dim your light and wants you to feel unsafe and scared.

If you're going to rid your life of evil, then you must focus solely on Jesus, love, and positive thoughts. When we focus on the power that love has, the energy vibration within us and around us becomes lighter, moving swiftly, just as it should. If your energy field is vibrating at a high level, you can feel it. Low vibrations make you feel tired, depressed, and you feel like you have a ball and chain dragging behind you. In some ways, you do. Negative energy is sticky, like a magnet that keeps piling itself on you. Negative energy has a hard time attaching itself to a moving and healthy energy field or chakra system. This system is the energy center that grounds your soul. Scientifically we can prove the energy field exists and this has nothing to do with religion and everything to do with human energy anatomy. We are energy and our soul is energy.

When it comes to embracing Jesus, you need to understand the depths of my experiences as I was delving into some profound, soulful moments, moments that the angels wanted me to experience.

It took me a while to understand the importance of connecting with Jesus. I needed experiences and these led me to learn and understand the meaning of Him. I learned how He plays a vital role within my life, with my gifts, my abilities, and about the critical role He has on the lives of many of us, if we allow Him to. I realized that in many of my experiences He was guiding me through the volume of my pain and misunderstandings of Him. My experiences, whether good or bad, were helping me discover my truth, with His truth. I needed to learn how to see Him differently than how I had done before. You see, Jesus was and always has been about love, acceptance, truth, understanding, faith, and safety. When you trust Him, your life will never be the same.

I never grew up in a strong Christian family, yet was drawn to the teachings of Jesus Christ. I was curious as a young child. My mom would send my sister and I to church on Sunday mornings and she always prayed with rosaries. I adopted her idea of prayer and have rosaries that I wear when I go into any place where people are experiencing spirit activity. I have rosaries that I use specifically for prayers before my readings and others for protection and healing for myself.

I sang in the church choir when I was eleven and was then baptized when I was forty, along with my husband and my second child. Things started to change for me at that time. Today, I understand why I was being asked by God to be baptized. It was going to help me with what God had in store for me, my future. He is my foundation. Before I start any communication with the spiritual realms, I pray to God first and I thank Him when I finish the reading. When I do a soul session, I always ask to have the Holy Spirit present so I know all information brought forward is for the highest good for the receiver.

Our experiences are life lessons we have chosen to live out within this lifetime. All life lessons help us discover our true self and learn how to become closer to God. Flaws in the ego are simply the soul learning how to return to God. Our soul strives to become one with God and this is why we have so much pain. The journey to become one with God is a holy one and any sacred path will always encourage evil opposition. Let's not forget Jesus's mission that lasted for forty days and forty nights. He was also tempted by the dark. Evil tries to keep us away from God and His love.

Here is my story with Jesus.

I was always looking for God and most of the time I never seemed to find Him. When I was going through the loss of my dad, I thought God had left me, forsaken me, and perhaps was even a little mad at me. But what had I done? I needed an explanation regarding why I couldn't see Him and why He wasn't returning my calls, so to speak.

One night while I was suffering in silence with emotional and spiritual pain, I lay on the couch looking through a window at the stars. I was alone at home, in my early twenties. The lights were turned off, a candle provided light, and I was feeling sorry for myself. I was recalling my previous pain and feeling depressed and unloved, feeling human I guess you could say. I once again reached out to see if He would answer my prayer but He never did. All I was asking was what He wanted from me. Why am I here? Is this all that there is? I know more, I need more, and I know I can have more. I pleaded out loud. I need your help! Please! A thick silence filled the air, as I patiently waited and listened, waiting to see if I could hear His voice or feel some answer, but I heard and felt nothing, only silence, and I never even felt the spirit world. A heaviness filled the air that night, the silence feeling deafening to my ears. That evening, I decided I wasn't going to call for a while. If God really wanted to talk to me, He had my number. He knew how to reach me and He knew how to find me. I was done reaching out, calling and searching for Him. At that time, God became a memory.

Even though I said I was done asking, I kept my soul open. Over the years I could feel the silence of His presence on many occasions, watching, waiting for something, but it was never clear why He was near. I always felt a barrier between me and Him. Eventually, I learned to listen with a silent and open mind to spirit. My angels stepped in and even my deceased loved ones were guiding me on my path, helping me walk the road that was to be my destiny. So, I listened and waited for many years, but there was still nothing. There was no sign from God. I have no idea what I was expecting to see, hear, or feel, that would show me that He was even close by.

One day while I was doing a medium reading, Jesus showed up right in the session. I was shocked. I guess it took Him a while to feel invited to do so. When you think about it, I'd pretty much tossed Him out of my life, shut the door on Him, and told Him I was done reaching out and asking for His advice. Consequently, I can't blame Him for being so up front with His message and getting my attention. But He wasn't there to say hello to me, but rather using me to say hello to my client. After that, the journey began.

Once I allowed Jesus to enter my personal life, He'd always show up at the most unusual times. I mean, is that not something that family members do? They show up unannounced, sometimes at the most inconvenient times. He quickly figured out ways to keep coming back into my life and believe me, He never missed a beat. He used other people too, to deliver messages to me because He knows I'm stubborn.

Over the years, I began to feel more and more comfortable when His spirit energy would enter my life. It wasn't a daily or a monthly thing but I can't ignore it when it happens. I've learned to listen when I feel His soul near me. I also had to come to terms with the fact that if His soul was coming into a reading then there must be an essential message coming forward for my client. When this happened, I learned to quickly gather my thoughts and figure out a way to get this message to my client without them feeling too uncomfortable or thinking I was crazy. After all, so many people believe what I do is weird, crazy, or evil.

In the reading, I was told that my client was praying to Him but became frustrated and blamed Him for everything painful that was going on in her life. She felt that if God or Jesus were real then He should take away her pain. She wasn't hearing Him or seeing the answers that were coming into her life from Him, but I could see them. I needed to show this to her and offer her a different perspective than the one she had at the time. Once all the validation was out of the way and the client's deceased loved ones had delivered their messages, it was Jesus' turn. He waited, always patiently, but I knew that I should never deny Him this opportunity. I graciously oblige every time. Jesus left as quickly as he'd arrived. It's incredible how the messages He told me to share with my client were exactly what the client needed to hear. They were usually in a fight with the dark and the light. Messages were always full of truth and love to help my clients move forward in their life. I can't even count how many times my clients have heard messages from Jesus through me and then decided to give Him another chance. Many chose to go back into a church, pick up their Bible and start reading it, and began to feel that there was hope in their lives once again.

I was asked by a friend what Jesus looked like and how He presented Himself to me. I can tell you that he always looks the same. He still glows with white light around Him and yes, He does have the long brown hair, beard, mustache, and is always wearing a long white robe or at least that's what it looks like to me. Please understand that Jesus isn't talking to me like other people talk to me, since the communication with the spirit world is very different to how we communicate in our physical world and it's very different with a divine soul. I think this is where some people get confused about spirit communication. I mainly feel Him and see Him within my mind's eye. When I see Him with my physical eye, which I have done, He has never spoken to me. I'm not having a one on one conversation with Him. That would be a little crazy and somewhat unnerving. I believe our physical body and our human mind couldn't take that kind of divine encounter lightly. I have realized that when you allow Jesus to enter into your world and He feels that you're ready, your life will never be the same. He takes control of your soul, in the right way, and you automatically become enlightened with love and peace. Your life will eventually become about Him. In reality, when the Holy Spirit touches your soul, your life will never be the same again. Dark days seem to diminish, you're not worried as much about things in your life that you want and need to control, your drive in this life becomes more related to helping to make the world a better place, and you begin to design a happier path with Jesus Christ in it.

The journey with Jesus isn't an easy one and takes time. It took me almost twenty years to gradually allow Him to enter into my world. I had to go through a lot of soul lessons until I could completely trust God. When I saw Him in pictures, I yearned for His closeness, His knowledge, and His love. What I had to figure out was that He was always near. I had to learn how to get out of my way, to experience His closeness. When I needed guidance, I'd find some form of literature or hear a song play on the radio. He even speaks through other people, just like the angels or even the deceased do. A person that I've never met before sometimes arrives with a message for me. They didn't know the message was for me, but I could feel there was a divine intervention connected to the message. Believe me, Jesus uses people and the angels to communicate with us. One day my husband and I were on our way to church and an old truck abruptly turned into our lane of traffic. My husband honked the car horn as this startled both of us. Written on the back of the vehicle in big white letters were the words 'Acknowledge the son of God 1-John 2:22-23'. I don't believe in coincidence. The angels were trying to get my attention with this divine message.

That same day when we were leaving church, my husband looked over at the side of the wall and asked if the picture displayed had always been there. It was a picture of Jesus within a stained glass window. I swear that when I looked at it, I thought I saw His eyes glow with a beautiful white light. Did the light shine through the window, just at the right time? Yes, as His eyes weren't really glowing. When I was leaving through the front door of the church, I looked up and saw another picture of Jesus, as clear as day. The light was shining so brightly that it caught my eye and it felt as if time had stood still. When the energy does this around me, I know from being a medium that the spirit world is sending me a divine message of love. It was a day of awareness, but little did I know that my experiences were just about to intensify. Thank goodness my husband had similar experiences. I might have thought I was losing my mind if he didn't understand it. This was also part of God's plan. No one is ever alone when they walk with Him.

One afternoon I was anxious about one of my sons. I prayed as I frequently do. I prayed for God and the angels to watch over him. I needed to leave and visit a client that day and it didn't seem right to cancel the appointment. I didn't want to leave my son either, but he was a competent teenager. I headed out and as I was sitting in my car, praying again, my right eye got a glimpse of someone. I quickly looked at the side of my house and I saw Him. There was a soul or a spirit that looked exactly like Jesus Christ did in my visions. This being that I believe was Jesus walked right through the wall of the house. I wasn't scared, although chills went through me and an incredible feeling of peace ran through my veins. This made my heart feel warm, still, and full of love. At that moment, I knew my son was going to be okay. When I arrived at my client's home, I sat in the car and called my son. I asked him how he was feeling. He told me that just after I'd left he fell asleep and woke up when I called him. This was unusual at the time. My son hadn't been sleeping well for months. He also told me not to worry about him and that everything was going to be okay and that he felt peaceful. God was working through him, I could feel it. After this brief encounter, I seemed to experience some frequent visitations from Jesus for a while. A message would come through and He would continue until I got the message. Yes, I know my life is a little strange. Being a sensitive and feeling and seeing divine energy is one of my gifts, so there's no reason to deny it.

One morning I needed to make some crucial decisions and some of the choices were part of my own personal and professional path. I was looking for my phone and again felt the presence of a powerful spiritual energy force. I found my phone and no word of a lie, the face of Jesus Christ was on the phone! Shocked would be an understatement. Now you might think this is crazy, but if the dead can manipulate the electrical currents within our location by flickering lights and draining cell phones batteries, surely Jesus could do the same. The image vanished just as quickly as it had arrived but it had been there just long enough to get my attention.

However, I was beginning to feel a little uncomfortable with all my experiences. I didn't know what to do with them and how I would tell my husband that Jesus was beginning to dominate his wife's life. How could I tell him not to worry, but I was changing? While I was experiencing all these weird and wacky moments, my life was becoming new and improved. I worried whether my husband would understand. What would the world think of me?

What would my friends think of me? I mean, I've been talking to the afterlife since I was a child and have conducted thousands of readings, giving validation to the living, but this was different. I feared that people would think I was crazy. Then I realized, well if that's what they think, okay. At least I'm a well-adjusted, happy, and loving person. Who cares about my belief in Jesus anyway? We're all programmed as a result of life's expectations and perceptions in one form or another. Yet I was afraid to let Jesus into my heart and soul. I thought perhaps I could keep Him at a distance, but eventually that didn't work out well for me.

I had to remember that I called Him and he finally answered my call. Was I to deny Him? He entered my life, enhancing it, bringing curiosity into my mind and healing my soul with each encounter. I wrote to Him through my journals, always letting Him know I was a fan and a follower. I attended functions at one of His houses of worship, and He had many homes along with a lot of followers and family members. However, people were scared of Him, although they never really knew Him. Some people fight for Him and others were killed who worshipped Him have been killed. He was a mysterious man and one I wanted to get to know, because He is not a man at all.

One evening as my husband and I were watching T.V. in bed, I turned on a Christian channel and we began to watch the show. It was one that we'd been watching for some time. I was getting ready to tell my husband of eighteen years, to share my story about my experiences with Jesus Christ. I was getting working up the nerve to share my insight into my life and explain all that was happening to me, but somehow I think he knew. He knew I was changing for the better, becoming happier, and he knew something was stirring inside my soul. Before I could say anything, my husband turned to me.

"You know, I have this deep desire to learn more about God, to reread the Bible and bring Jesus closer into my life," he said.

I was a little shocked. Did God have his number too? Was my husband next? While I was excited and happy, I also knew that this journey wasn't going to be an easy one for me and new challenges were going to emerge. However, I kept reminding myself that whatever I was to experience would be for my highest good. Whatever I was to learn, I was to write.

Because of Jesus Christ and his teachings, I want to be a better person. Now that's something to think about. I share this with you because I personally believe there has been so much misunderstanding when it comes to Jesus and His teachings. Heaven wants your soul when you pass because that is the place in which you'll have eternal peace. Heaven is your home and where your soul belongs. Jesus is in heaven. He is a spirit being and He wants you. If you do want to allow Jesus into your life, don't get involved with a church that doesn't fit your style of thought. Find a Church or a community that teaches the love of Jesus and learn how His spirit can positively affect your life. So why did Jesus show up so much in my life? He wanted me to know I could trust in Him, call on Him when I needed, and believe me, I've called Him many times. He also reminds me that I should never lose my faith, no matter what experiences may come forward in my life or what people may say to me about what I do, for I'll be with Him once again. And best of all, I have two fathers and two mothers in heaven, because Mother Mary is very close to my heart too.

CHAPTER FIVE

~

What's Happening In Heaven?

The deceased have shown me that there are many levels in heaven and everything the dead speak about is essential. Yet they won't tell me everything about heaven, as they're not allowed to. This has to do with the rules of heaven that govern our world. Some things are sacred and kept a secret from those on Earth. The goal of the soul is to reach the ultimate level in heaven, the level where one lives eternally with God. There seem to be many levels within heaven, each corresponding to the soul life lessons, meaning that each level is unique to the soul. I've also seen that each soul has free will, like the living do, and a soul can heal or decide not to improve itself. Most choose the latter.

I never believed it before, but I'm a firm believer now. It's a choice if you want to reincarnate too. It won't happen automatically and if it does, it's done solely to enhance the soul, so you can become closer to God. You may find this interesting, but reincarnation is rare and not everyone has a past life. The deceased I've spoken to have rarely talked about past lives or reincarnation and I've talked to thousands of them. Believe me, you don't have to have a T.V. show in order to receive exclusive information from the afterlife. Remember, the ego doesn't reside in heaven, just in the physical world. I've been told several times within readings that people have lived previous lives. I therefore know this is real and perhaps when I'm talking to them there are souls that don't know whether they'll reincarnate, so they don't talk about it. If reincarnation does take place, it happens much, much later in the heavenly realms. It probably takes about a hundred or two hundred life years for one to reincarnate. When all your family is in heaven and you've met your deceased loved ones and have done your healing, perhaps it's then that you make the decision. However, from what the dead have told me, it's a choice. I guess we won't discover the truth until it's our own time.

However, do be very suspicious if a psychic or medium tells you that your loved ones aren't available to speak as they've reincarnated. Maybe they have but it's more likely they haven't. If you hear this a lot, the medium is either not getting the information from the other side or is dodging something. Not all mediums are real mediums. Sometimes they are what I call surface level mediums and are only getting a quick glance at the deceased or even your memories. Some mediums use telepathy and aren't talking to the dead at all.

I've always found it strange when during readings I bring forward someone that passed a long time ago. In such cases, my clients usually agree that they know the person but point out that they passed away a long time ago. Or they tell me that they never knew them and wonder why they are coming through. I then have to agree and inform the client that although they passed a long time ago they're still in heaven and they know them. I then tell them the truth, that their loved one wants to talk to them and say hello. The dead want to talk. Your deceased loved ones want you to know you're watched over. You never know who will come through. You might have one or two people talking or you might have up to fifteen people or more talking. This has happened many times in my private readings. During a reading, a deceased loved one may come in to say hello, one may enter that's really chatty, and one may be quiet. You just never know what will happen when you're talking to your deceased loved ones, so remember that reincarnation doesn't always happen. And if your loved ones want to speak, which they always do, they will if they can.

It seems that on most occasions the deceased don't even acknowledge the existence of reincarnation when I am doing a reading. Now I'm not saying reincarnation isn't real, but I have been told from the spirit world it's not of importance to our current life. They have told me we are to concentrate on our life today. If we worry too much about a life we don't remember, we may miss the true meaning regarding our reason for being here today. Angels don't reincarnate into this world and neither would Jesus or His disciples. Why would they? We may never know the truth.

While I'm not trying to upset anyone, I do think there is more going on with past lives and the ages of our soul than people may have previously considered. If past life therapy has helped you, I'm happy for you. I no longer entertain this healing modality anymore. There doesn't seem to be any long-term benefit to it. I wrote about this is my first book, *A Soul's Journey*. But spirit felt that it was important to mention it with more understanding in this second book. If you were wondering why the deceased don't talk about this much and why we're not talking about the topic in this book, it's because there's not enough evidence to identify this as the truth. Now I'm sure some people want to express their thoughts to me about what I'm writing, because they're believers and have all sorts of positive stories. However, I write what I believe and what I've been taught from heaven. And like I said before, the dead have lots to say.

One day while I was writing, my father briefly showed up. I could feel him and sense him. Even though I didn't see him with my physical eyes this time, I saw him within my mind. When we see spirit in our minds and feel all sorts of energy around us, it's our loved ones communicating telepathically with us. I closed my eyes and allowed his communication to enter into mine. He told me he loved me, was proud of me, and that he wanted to stop in to say hello. He then proceeded to tell me that my uncle, who was sick at the time, would be passing within a day or two, which he did. Even though I knew my uncle was ill, I had no idea how sick he was. I hadn't seen him physically for over twenty years and no one had recently been talking about him. My dad was getting ready to greet him and escort him into heaven or was part of the team that helps family enter into heaven. My mother-in-law did the same thing to me. I kept feeling her and seeing images of her in my mind. I actually kept hearing some of the words she would often say. I told my husband.

"I don't know why but your mom's spirit has been around over the last day or so," I told him.

Two days later, my husband received a message that his cousin had died. This would be the nephew of my mother-in-law. She was getting ready to take him to the other side and had decided to do some visiting beforehand.

Our loved ones visit us, most of the time discreetly. They have opportunities to see us and check on how we are doing. However, they're not allowed to interfere too much within our lives. Free will dictates that it's a big no no on the other side to interfere too much with the living, that is if you want to remain in the right place that peacefully allows you to visit the earthly realm. This rule is the same for readings too. When a deceased loved one speaks they first need to provide me with specific information. I test the spirit in many ways. Once they provide specific validation and my client confirms it, I let them speak freely. They love to tell me all about their lives. They show us the occasions when they visited their loved ones by communicating with me about things that have happened. They do this in order to provide reassurance to the living. Your loved ones bring through their personalities and I encourage them to do this, as this brings forward strong validation. You see, you aren't able to look up a character on the internet. You can't make up a personality either, not if you have never met them before. As a physical medium, I often take on the demeanour, facial characteristics, and movements of the deceased. This happens from time to time when you're a physical medium, but it's draining for the physical body. The environment

47

has to be free of negativity and skeptics. Having spirit manifest around you can also be dangerous to the soul.

One evening I was conducting a sacred circle. This is when I bring around ten or fifteen people together. I have them sit in a circle and I allow their loved ones to come forward to me so I can provide random messages to them. This is a small group reading. However, when we sit in a circle, the energy becomes intense and very healing. In small groups it's also much easier to take on the personality of the deceased and even make gestures and have facial expressions that resemble them. I was told from the other side that the departed enjoy this circle too because of the healing that takes place in a small group setting and I let the spirit speak. The soul of the deceased seems to feel more able to make connections with the living. I'm not saying it won't happen in a large group reading, because it has. Yet our loved ones enjoy small and intimate settings too, as they get to talk more.

Spirit communication is about love and healing and this is why heaven and God allow this to happen. Specific information should never be requested or demanded and this is important. If we're demanding particular information to come through from our loved ones, we're creating a harsh energetic environment that isn't conducive to the heavenly realms. A demanding or negative demeanour can entirely close communication with your loved ones. The energy of all involved is also very important to the success of the messages. If you have low vibration or have been drinking alcohol or taking drugs recently your energy will be low. If you're closed off, angry, or don't want to be where you are, your reading will close down. Your energy matters to the success of your messages. Your loved ones and I can feel the energy of your thoughts.

The best way I can describe talking to the deceased is that the soul in heaven begins to merge with my soul. It feels sacred to me and humbling. I've always left the door open and trust that if something is imperative for my client to know, my angels step in and tell me that we need to change the reading a bit, as a soul message is coming through for them. It's so important to let any spirit communication unfold as it should, with no expectations and no demanding of information. Surrender to the understanding that your loved ones will provide what you need. That's the energy in heaven.

I've seen that once the soul enters heaven, it takes time for them to realize that they've passed. Part of their healing is to visit their funeral service or celebration of life. They take time and watch over their loved ones and they do this with God and His angels or with the angel that's been appointed to watch over them, taking them to the life review room or let's say level. There's lots of effort and energy being brought forward when you pass and when you're born. When you have your life review, you'll see the things you've done wrong within your life. You'll get time to review and see how you could have done things better or differently. You may experience how other people acted and explore how they felt when your actions took place. This is a tedious and very soul-changing task. To examine the pain of another is never fun. Relieving pain, including yours, is never an easy task either. One significant thing I want to mention is that there is no time in heaven. Time is human made, whereas time in heaven is different and is there as and when we need it. They only need time to heal, but this isn't time as we understand it, measured by clocks.

I'm often asked how much time must elapse after a loved one has passed before I can speak with them. Well, I've talked to deceased loved ones as recently as two days after the passing and also with those that have passed more than fifty years before the reading. It all depends on the deceased, what has happened, and where they are in the realms of heaven. If the soul has had a traumatic passing or committed suicide, they may be harder to reach at first, but I can guarantee that they will pay a visit, if they have some vital information to share with the loved one or person in front of me. It seems the dead can indeed communicate very quickly after their passing, if needed.

The ego doesn't exist on the other side. The ego is only part of the physical world. When the deceased is taken to see their reviews, they eventually see their life with a healthy consciousness. It's going to take time for the earthly memories, grief, pain, anger, and frustration to leave them. Once all this has gone, their personality hasn't changed and they're still the same person, but slightly different. They no longer carry anger, hate, pain, or sickness within them. They remember this but don't seem to feel it anymore. They are therefore pain-free and can now think clearly. Again, we have no idea how long it takes the deceased to move through their pain. Time is irrelevant in heaven, healing is what's important. However, when I do a reading the soul comes through as very aware of their physical world, the pain they caused, their happiness, and the memories of their life. They retain their personality, so if they liked to have fun in the physical world, they still have fun in heaven and they show me this. Our loved ones love to laugh and remember the good old times when they were alive. They are serious when needed, especially when they or you are going through a healing during your session.

There's a serious side to all of this too. When loved ones come through to speak, they're using this opportunity to say hello to you. They're also using this time to heal their soul. This soul healing allows them to reach certain levels within heaven, so we know that healing and talking to our deceased loved ones is important. Heaven has an important plan for spirit communication. A lot happens within a reading and it's never used for evil or negative intentions, not during my readings. When the deceased use this time for healing purposes, at first they always give me specific information about what needs to heal. I'll also determine if it should be spoken about first. I consult with my spiritual team and when all is good, they can speak about whatever they feel is essential to them and their loved ones. I trust all the information that's coming through is the information my client needs to hear.

When a loved one wants to provide you with healing and the communication is going to heal their soul, there's a specific symbol they place on their heart. When I see this symbol, I know to be ready for a great and extremely important healing that's about to take place. This is when, if needed, I ground myself quickly to make sure I don't feel too much emotional pain. I tell my client that there's an essential healing message coming forward for them, their loved one has a healing sign on them, and that this is important for their healing and my client's. I always ask them if they'd like to proceed and talk with their loved one.

I might look calm and collected in a reading, but a great deal is happening energetically and within my mind. As a medium, I have a huge responsibility not only to deliver truthful, in-depth messages, but to honour the significance of the moment for both parties, the living person and the soul in the afterlife. And believe it or not, when a considerable healing is coming forth, the angels are watching. They watch over me to ensure that I'm not getting too tired and that the soul of the deceased isn't taking too much of my energy. My angels always make sure I'm never put in danger from the spirit world. However, on a negative note, the living may do things that can bring danger to a medium. This is why I've tried hard never to bring my ego into the reading. If I have to tell my client that their loved ones prefer not to answer the questions, I can comfortably and promptly say so. I say it with a clear conscience. The living may not like this, but they're not the ones putting their physical health at risk, as I am. However, they may be putting their soul at risk, because like I said God and His angels are always watching.

One day I was getting ready to do a reading for a male client. Even though most of my clients are female, I've seen an increase over the years where men are feeling more comfortable and willing to speak with their deceased loved ones, which I think is wonderful. While I was preparing for the reading, the energy felt off. These feelings are usually a heads up from the spirit world. I told my husband that I wanted him close by, at least accessible by phone if needed. The man arrived and his energy was intense. I felt anger around him, not grief. I always try and remain heart-centerd and make sure I come from a place of love all times during my sessions. After all, my job is to deliver messages from deceased loved ones. I began to bring forward his mother, all the information verified, but he seemed confused. I asked him why and he said that his mother was Catholic and never believed in mediums and talking with the dead. I simply informed him that things often seem to change when one enters into the afterlife and that she was with us.

51

I proceeded to provide more information, after which his energy changed. The deceased mother backed away quickly, disconnected from me, and he demanded to know the name of the demon I was bringing forward. I was shocked.

"Look," I said. "If you're going to think this is a demon and not your mom then you need to leave this reading. Your negativity is also seriously impacting the reading, not to mention it's not good for me to continue the reading within this hostile environment you are creating."

He looked at me, smiled and said that he knew this. This is a rare occurrence but it has happened. This man might have felt that what he was doing was okay, or strangely enough, thought he was doing something good for the more significant cause. However, he was doing something very wrong. It was terrible for his soul. His loved one might never have come back and spoke again. But more than anything his actions were recorded on his soul for all the angels to see. We pay for our actions here on Earth, whether we like it or not.

What I'm about to talk about is from the deceased, not from my beliefs. I'm being a messenger here and sharing with you what I've been told in a reading from people who have passed over. I was once doing a reading for a young man and his father came through. We went through the usual meet and greet and the father letting me know how he'd passed. I felt how he'd passed away, but he seemed odd about the passing. And then he said that he wasn't proud of it but there was no indication of suicide, which always looks different to me in a reading. I told his son that the man was taking responsibility for his passing and had to work through it on the other side. This means that he needed to heal from what he'd done. I asked the son if he understood the message and he said that he did, which was good because at the time I was unable to understand it. As long as it made sense to the receiver, all was good. What I found out later is that the father was an assisted suicide and he had to pay the price for taking his own life before it was his time. You see, the soul hangs on for a reason, even when sick. Declaring that you wish to refuse any resuscitation is okay, but asking to die before you're supposed to pass is a no no. Again, I'd delivered the message. It wasn't coming from me, but from the dead.

I remember when my mother-in-law passed she was having a hard time breathing while she was in the hospital bed, waiting for her soul to get ready for the afterlife. It was a painful thing to watch and I could feel and see her pain. She never spoke during this time, but I knew she could hear us. My husband and I were at the hospital. I called my eldest son and told him we were going to stay a little longer as we thought that she might not make it another night. My son became upset and said he needed to say goodbye. I explained that she would be able to hear him, but couldn't respond, but that he should say what he needed to say. I then put the phone to her ear. I could not hear everything, but I watched her breathing and I knew she could hear him. Her breathing changed when he was talking. I also saw a movement within her arm and hand. That conversation will be one of the most critical discussions my son will remember. The family asked why she was hanging on and that she should go. I explained that it wasn't her time and that she was waiting for her sister. When her sister arrived the next day she told my mother-in-law that it was time to go and she peacefully passed away. I'm not only proud of her but am also so grateful that she chose to wait and let God carry her when it was her time. God and your soul have a plan. We were estranged from my mother-in-law for a time and my kids had unfinished business. This conversation brought lots of closure to one of them. My other son was still very young and processed the memories and the passing differently. Now my older son harbours no ill feelings. As I write, I can feel her spirit close to me. I can feel a healing is moving through me as I process this memory and write about it. In essence, I'm thanking her in my own way for hanging on as long as she did.

When someone is ill and will soon be passing, they often see their loved ones in spirit. They see their loved ones that have passed on. Our loved ones frequently visit to see how we are doing. The closer one is to death, the more regularly one may be viewing the deceased. The healthy can see them too and yet many people don't see their loved ones at all. I believe that has a lot to do with our minds. Our left-brain protects us from what we are witnessing or blocks it out if it's going to cause us distress. That's why you sometimes can't see your loved ones in spirit after they pass or you quickly recognize them but then may not see them for a while. It's different for everyone. I mentioned earlier that they aren't allowed to interfere with your life or cause you distress if they're visiting from heaven. If they're visiting from hell, well that would be a different book.

I have also spoken to souls that left their earthly life way before their time as a result of abortion or miscarriage. When a soul steps forward, they have a symbol indicating that they were lost before their time, but in reality, it was their time. With regards to abortions, I've spoken to these souls and they want their parents to let go of the pain or any fear they have. It seems as if some forgiveness is brought forward to the living, as the deceased or unlived soul gets an opportunity to say hello. They want to express that they know why they were aborted or left the womb early and will see you in heaven when it's your time.

How does heaven look? Well, there are different levels in heaven. The top-level is with God and all strive to get there, although not all do. So the deceased work their way up. They do this by healing. They need to look at their past and see how they could have done things better or differently. In a schoolroom in heaven healing takes precedence over anything else. Mediumship is so vital to the living and the dead. For example, I had a father show up in a reading and could feel this was going to be an in-depth session, full of healing. He showed me the healing sign and started giving me his validation and then we were ready to open up some old wounds for him and my client. I saw how my client had experienced rape at the hands of her father. He did some bad things and needed to explain and apologize to her. I strive to feel no emotion during a reading, as I am merely the person delivering the message of healing. Him talking to his daughter and apologizing was helping both of their souls. When a person comes through and reveals they know what has gone on within their child's life and it involves something like rape, this can entail an emotional reading. I had a mother come forward and tell her daughter, my client, that she knew about the abuse. However, the daughter never told her when she was alive and only found out after she passed. Remember, I know nothing and all the information is coming from the deceased.

Sometimes when I open up the door to heaven, I see a hallway and the loved ones start to move forward toward me, if they haven't already arrived before the reading. Remember this doorway is coming from the in-between. When this is happening, I see pets who are waiting to speak or sometimes deceased loved ones come toward me with flowers, usually varieties that mean something to the reading. Cakes with candles always mean that loved ones are coming forward to celebrate a birthday, an anniversary, or something they or the family will be celebrating soon if not currently. My number one rule is that the deceased loved one mustn't bring forward the cake image unless the event is happening within ninety days. Otherwise, it could be too vague and I like information that can be validated. I receive smells of perfume or flowers, if that means something to the people who are with me. If the deceased was a heavy smoker I can smell the cigarettes or cigars. Whatever they want to share is fine with me. However, they're always careful about the images they reveal to me. In one reading a man come forward to speak with his daughter and spent a lot of time watching a woman dance. I was grateful that he only showed me a woman in a bathing suit wearing high heels. I understood the message quickly and the image soon disappeared. I mean, no one wants to see a naked person in a reading. Yes, they're always wearing something. Sometimes I can only see their face and facial features that stand out. If they wore a uniform when they were alive, they show me their uniform at some point during the reading. If they loved to dress up and wear jewelry, I see it all. If they were more casual, I see casual garments. I've found that when they show me what they're wearing they're also teaching me about their personality. If I could only draw, I'd be able to create some beautiful portraits for the deceased with what they show me. I do draw stick people and outlines of objects, but it doesn't do justice to what I see and what they show me. One of the strangest things I felt was when they were showing me their beard. I could experience if their beard was long or short. I felt this on my face, as if hair was growing on me.

As a medium, I've realized that the other side uses my abilities to do good. They use this time wisely for healing purposes. This is really what real mediumship is all about. The other side was telling me about the importance of my gift. I needed to make sure I took this ability seriously and needed to do everything in my power to portray my truth to the world. What I've always heard is that I must protect it, so I do my best. Being a medium isn't about hosting workshops to increase your psychic connections. It's not about holding seances or trying to tell everyone you're the best in the business and that you can teach anyone to be a medium or to become a psychic. It's also not about removing voodoo spells and using witchcraft. Being a medium is about healing and most importantly to inform people in our world that life lives on after death. The dead are always trying to tell us the importance of living life the best way we can. If you want to learn how to connect, learn to heal your pain first.

I have done readings for people that were adopted and never got to talk to their mom, but their mom showed me she was very much in their lives from the other side. There's no measure for that kind of healing. The dead want to tell me their story. Sometimes the dead divulge health information to me regarding their living loved ones health and even give clarification about their own health when they were alive.

You see, listening to the dead can bring relevant information to the living. The message is to help both souls heal. This is heaven's intention for what I do. I always ask the deceased to show me what they're doing in heaven. Interestingly, they show me their memories, things they like to do and the places they enjoy attending. This information is always verified by my client. The deceased person then tells me that they visit places that are close to their heart and see the people that once loved them, checking how they are doing. They reminisce and visit old friends. I've seen the deceased show me pets that have passed and are with them. They tell me they're still walking the dog, just in heaven. They visit the places where they liked to walk or hike. They may also sit at home and watch their favourite T.V. show, all while sitting in their favourite chair that's still in the living room. Visiting the living world like this takes place when they're at a reasonable level in heaven and no longer require much healing.

One day I was doing a family reading and the two women had the same close friend. While I was finishing up talking with their loved one, I asked if there was anyone else they wanted to hear from in heaven. Family members always speak first in my readings then close loved ones and friends come through. However, just before I was getting ready to close the session, I suddenly had a young man in his mid-twenties come forward, wearing an outfit normally seen in Japan.

"I'm sorry, am I too late for the reading?" he said. "I was in another country visiting, as I loved to travel."

I looked at the two women and they began to laugh. I asked if this made sense to them and they nodded and told me that they'd been waiting for him to come through. His delay was no surprise to them, as he loved to travel and wanted to visit other places around the world before he passed away. These two woman considered this man to be one of their closest friends. However, he never got the chance and they told me that he was late for everything. I reassured them that he was still the same. As I was just about to close the reading, he told me to tell them that he was travelling to the places he desired to go but was doing this in the world of spirit. So, can we go to other countries after we die? I believe we can if we're on the right level to do so.

Heaven looks beautiful to me, but I've seen what it's like for them and each person seems to have a different view, although they do the same things there. Heaven is like a school for the soul. Spirit or deceased loved ones are on Earth far more often than one might think and so are angels.

One day I was doing a reading for a woman and her father came through. We did the usual validation then he began to speak. The deceased always seem to know what you need to hear and if they were a talker in the physical world, they would be a talker in the reading most of the time, unless someone else is trying to speak more than them. The same usually goes with the quiet, shy type. Personality remains the same after we die. This man was a talker for sure. He talked so fast that I had to ask him to slow down and he was so excited to be able to speak with his daughter. He told me to tell her that heaven was real and that he was busy golfing with his friend. His daughter began to laugh and cry at the same time. Her dad was with his best friend and they golfed all the time. I was shown the golf course, what it looked like, so it seems that they visited the places they loved. Are they golfing? No, not really. Maybe each of us gets an opportunity to plan their own heaven and their soul moves around within the mirrors of memories or energy. And maybe it's simply their own treasured memories that they decide to speak about.

I have seen parts of heaven and when this happened I saw an ocean that I'd never seen before, unusual yet beautiful animals in the water, and a sky with colours that I can't duplicate no matter how hard I've tried. I've been shown this by the deceased and on one or two occasions during my dreams. I was also shown a place where souls wait in a level within the in-between. This place is where souls decided to go back to Earth or proceed to heaven. I was shown this when I was under anaesthetic during one of my operations. I was seeing what God and His angels needed me to see.

I've spent years researching and genuinely understanding my abilities or gift. I've come to terms with the fact that not all will believe and that's okay. It was vital for me to understand my path, as we all have a different calling. Even a medium will be more than just a medium and they need to find out what their calling is. There's always more. More experiences, more learning, more understanding, and more teachings to receive from the other side, if you're open to it. It depends on what you need in your life and what you need to know to help you on your path.

I've had many interesting things happen during a reading. A deceased mother I was speaking with was Catholic and she spoke these words to me in a reading.

"While we (the spirit world) are glad you're thanking the angels, you must start thanking God first. He's the one that allows this to happen."

She was referring to spirit communication. She had a rather stern demeanour so ever since that day I give thanks to Jesus and God before and after a reading. You see, spirit is always teaching me and you don't want to argue with the dead.

On another occasion, a father was speaking to me from heaven and told me that the man upstairs was happy with what I was doing. I was a little shocked by this comment, to say the least. He knew I was worried and needed to deliver a message to me from the spirit world during his reading. It felt like a domino effect. Heaven does see and it seems our angels or even God speaks to the deceased and might just tell them what you need. Heaven is one big happy family.

All this kind of communication happens after all the validation has come through. There's an order to all this talk and it's important stuff. As a medium, I feel as if I'm working for heaven.

There's a mystery to what I do and a mystery to the other side as well. I've always had an interest in the human mind. At one point in my life, I wanted to work on criminal cases as a psychologist. Understanding why people do what they do, especially criminals, has always fascinated me. Actually there are lots of things in this world that fascinate me. However, it took some time for me to realize why the criminal mind fascinated me. It's mostly connected to my life calling. To understand the mind and all the levels within it allows me to be a better spirit communicator.

When I conducted my very first group event about twelve years ago, a boy that was missing came through. He was the cousin of the female client in front of me. I wrote about this in my first book, *A Soul's Journey*, as this was my first missing person encounter. I've done numerous readings where a loved one that was murdered would come through and needed to explain their story. I've spoken to deceased loved ones where unexplained events would be explained during a reading. Each time I did these kinds of sessions, the client never informed me that the reading was going to be about a missing person or a murder. This is the best way to approach this kind of reading. When I know nothing, spirit gives me everything. These cases can be hard to work on as I feel everything in a reading, the pain of the living and the pain of the dead.

When I was in grade nine, I had to do an essay, which could be on any topic I wanted. At that time, I wanted to write an essay about men who raped. This was a strange topic for a grade nine girl to be interested in but my teacher was fascinated with my essay. He gave me an excellent mark and was very impressed. I got a high grade and was proud, to say the least. I spent hours investigating in the library and getting my hands on any book that allowed me to enter the minds of male criminals that were convicted of rape. At the time, I didn't understand my fascination, but I also felt as if something or someone was guiding me to write it and I never questioned this. It would be years later when I came upon this memory once again, only to realize that my school had once been a school for boys that were in trouble with the law. Knowing what I know now, I wonder if someone from the afterlife was telling me their story. Perhaps my writing about it was allowing him to heal. I may never know the truth, but it makes you wonder about the power of the deceased spirit, the need for healing, and perhaps how heaven knows exactly how to facilitate this healing for the souls in the afterlife.

The deceased have a story too and the dead need to heal and to be heard. I have a theory that perhaps my desire to write about specific topics might be caused by spirit communicating to me, wanting me to share their story or at least help another with their earthly actions. The spirit world is not only fascinating, heaven is a world all of its own.

Since the spirit world is always around when I open that door, I've had to learn and watch how I feel on the morning or day when I have readings. I learned that it's not unusual to feel pain in areas of my body and realize the deceased were feeling this too. Was their pain reflecting on me? Was my connection to spirit happening hours before and my physical mind not making the connection? As an empath I've learned to be wise to my feelings throughout the day, as I do sense spirits before the readings start. I watch the types of people and readings I'm engaged in. Spirit is trying to indicate where heaven needs me and I must remain open to work on all levels of spirit communication when required. Remember, I feel the dead want to tell their story, cases need to be solved so the dead can rest, and investigations, whether paranormal or otherwise, need to be done. People need to heal from grief and they can do this by talking to their loved ones and sometimes people need essential information from the spirit world. This is heaven and it's a beautiful, restful, busy place. Heaven gives the deceased time to heal and an environment for their soul that allows them to learn how to get closer to God. For the living, the powers of heaven allow you to receive a sense of healing, just by being able to talk with your deceased loved ones and this is what's up in heaven.

CHAPTER SIX

~

Is Evil Or Negative Energy Real?

I know some people are going to have a tough time with this topic, but evil, negative energy, attachments, and demons are real. I'm pretty sure Satan is too, I've just never met him, thank goodness! Sometimes when we learn we must step out of our comfort zone and I really stepped out of my comfort zone on this one.

One of the most challenging aspects of being a writer, or approaching writing with an investigative mindset, is that I've had to experience exactly what it is I'm writing about. I'm also writing based on my personal experiences. I'm very grateful for the knowledge I've gained over the years regarding mental health issues. I needed to learn about this part of the human mind because the truth is some people that have witnessed evil have a mental health issue. Unfortunately, I've had a small number of people visit me regarding house hauntings, feeling oppressed, or experiencing attacks from some evil force, only to find out in a session that they were suffering from a mental health issue. When this happens, I ask the client if they have recently been suffering any health issues or have been under severe emotional stress. I only ask these questions if I get a heads up from spirit and no one seems to have any problems answering them. Remember, I can feel health issues within the energy soul of people. I know for a fact that paranormal experiences are real and it's rare that it's a health issue. However, I also attract people that need healing, it's what I do. So I do what needs to be done. Spirit will always tell me the truth, meaning that if their experience is real I need to look more into their situation. Are they being haunted? Do they have a negative attachment on them? Is their location haunted? Do they have haunted objects within their possession? I need to further understand what it is they're experiencing and where this experience is coming from.

The experiences I talk about may leave you feeling uncomfortable and rest assured I sometimes feel uncomfortable speaking about this topic. It's interesting how many people become somewhat agitated, angry, fearful, or downright strange when I talk about evil and negative energy. I can see what's going on within their mind. They're wondering if I'm crazy. Did I lose my mind? Remember, people are often afraid of what they don't understand and sometimes they think people who talk about it are mad. Believe me, no one wants to be told they have an attachment walking around with them, one that's causing chaos within their life. I've had to learn to work through this. I've had strange looks when I speak about evil. It's human nature to avoid what it is we fear and I have to wonder if this fear is deep within our soul because we know its truth yet choose not to see it for what it is. Consequently, I've learned to keep my mouth shut and weed the people out of my life that prefer not to help me grow or accept me for who I am. However, I'm exploring these things in this book because even though some of this might sound crazy, I am not. I'm very aware of my surroundings, spiritual energy, and the spirit world. I must share what I have seen and experienced, because I'm not the only one and am here to help you.

There are different kinds of evil within this world and I've had many spiritual and paranormal experiences beginning when I was around five years old. Some stories I'll share with you in this book, some I'll wait to include in my next book. It's always a struggle trying to figure out what I should write and what I should wait on. I have so much information sitting in my head from all of my experiences. It can be a little overwhelming at times.

Today, I can see why Jesus was trying to get my attention. His ministry seemed to focus on deliverance and removing demons from other people's souls or out of their minds. The Old Testament seemed to be more about sin and temptation against the word of God, the New Testament about identifying and combatting evil, or at least that's how I see it. Our world is very different today to how it was when Jesus was engaged in his ministry and ancient languages were also very different to those spoken widely today.

Words used in the past may be replaced today with something else, giving them an entirely different meaning. I might remove evil or help get it out of you, but I don't consider myself to be an exorcist. I do have ways to encourage evil to leave your life. There are demons of the mind, the soul, and there are negative attachments, negative energy, and residual energy within our world. My ability to hear and see evil has helped me and others throughout my time as a medium. In 2017, around the time when Jesus kept showing up in my life, my desire to know and understand Him was powerful. I was seriously considering entering into ministry. It wasn't a random thought and I was very serious about the idea. Today, I study theology and psychology whenever I can. It's important to me and goes hand in hand with what I do. The experience I had earlier with Jesus made me realize that perhaps He was guiding me toward Him. I wanted to experience everything I could that was connected to Jesus. I began to volunteer helping another minister and attended church regularly. I still attend as much as I can today. I wasn't afraid of making a change or becoming a minister. I was more concerned about whether this was indeed the path that I should follow. I was certain that God wanted me to talk to people in heaven, to help others through grief, and somehow unconventionally rid others of negative attachments within their lives, which is sometimes not as easy as one may think.

I finally realized that God was working through me and Jesus was my anchor in life and in my work as a medium. I was healing and purifying my soul through the knowledge I'd gained through my experiences with Jesus.

I've always sensed evil or negative energy, even as a child. Children are very intuitive. I believe children are closer to God but as we grow older many fall away from Him. It took years for me to understand why I could sense evil and negative energy around people, along with their negative thoughts around and within them. I had this ability because of my empathic gift. When I look back, I think I made people feel uncomfortable when I was young. They sensed something different about me and it confused them. This is what happens when our expectations don't correspond with our thoughts. We have fear of what we don't understand and this word empath or someone's ability as an empath was never spoken about. Now, we'll examine some of the scary stuff. I should point out that many empaths are actually drawn to the paranormal, as they can sense good and bad energy or spirits. God is showing them where He needs them to be.

On my first scary visual encounter with evil, I was doing a Reiki session with a girl I'd only met a couple of times before so I didn't know much about her life. When my hands hovered over her back, I saw a female that looked, to put it bluntly, evil. She was angry and I pulled my hands away quickly but she sensed this. I should mention that this wasn't a paying client. I was merely practicing my Reiki skills and barely knew her. She asked if I was okay and I think she sensed my fear too.

"Well I'm not trying to scare you, but I think you have an attachment over your lower back," I said. "This attachment got angry when I tried to put healing energy to it. Do you have lower back problems?"

She replied that she'd been suffering for years with lower back, since she was a teenager. However, she explained that she'd never told anyone and made adjustments within her life when her back became painful. Of course, she denied believing it was an attachment and

I certainly didn't push the issue. However, I did do a releasement prayer quietly and she told me later that her back pain disappeared for months and I never talked with her about it again. She was a very positive and pleasant person. This was my first lesson on how pain can manifest into visual attachments and even become secure from our own will.

When I had my second encounter, I began to wonder what it was all about. Why was I seeing negative energy and dark attachments on people and was all this even possible? I was doing another Reiki session on a woman. This was a paying client and I found a negative energy attachment hidden deep within her knee joint. I would call this a memory attachment. This memory was of someone she'd once loved and she was still angry and hurt about. She was carrying her anger in her knee. This anger created an attachment that was stopping her from moving forward in her current relationship and causing her unexplained knee pain. The pain was intense for me. I could feel it. I also could see what the man looked like and the client confirmed that my description was correct. I felt his personality and his anger. When I began to pull away from her energy body and started to pull this energy force from her, I began to feel nauseated. I used specific symbols and put light energy into the knee. However, I was a newbie at this energy thing and was trying to follow the guidance from my intuition. I've now learned to do things differently and have a spiritual helper, one who works with me from the other side.

While I was being told to be careful from my spiritual guide it took me a while to learn how to protect myself during these types of sessions. After my client left, I ran to the bathroom and vomited. It was intense. I was ridding my body of all the toxic energy. Somehow I absorbed some of it and that was a harsh lesson to learn. I spoke to my client about this and coached her through her healing. She was forever grateful and told me that she had a feeling that it was going to be an intense healing, but she didn't expect just how deep it was going to be. Her knee caused no further problems or pain and her current relationship was much better.

As my journey began with energy healing and learning to tap into the in-between, I started to notice grey or smoky energy around some people. This was usually hovering over one of their energy centers. The heart, the mid-section, and the throat seemed to be prevalent in some people. Seeing this energy form can happen in a reading, a healing, or even during a coaching session. It occurs when I focus on reading the spiritual energy around people and they've given me permission to do so. I've seen this source of spiritual energy since I was a child. We carry a lot of our pain in our energy body, which will eventually enter into the physical body if not properly healed. I learned over the years how to deal with what I was experiencing and on most occasions never told anyone that I saw an attachment on them. Many people in my life haven't believed the things I have experienced and this can be disheartening. My clients don't have a problem with it because I'm an integral part of their healing. Many experiences regarding attachments, negative energy, or seeing evil entities are only truly understood when one experiences it first-hand. I'm still working on this. I feel that even after so many years, I'm still a work in progress, as most of us probably are.

Over the years, I've learned that if you disrupt Satan's kingdom he's going to try to disturb you, so be strong. Because of my ability related to spiritual discernment, by which I know and sense good and evil spirits, my life took an exciting turn one day. I'd been doing house clearing and blessings for years and had many unusual experiences before I decided to delve further into the paranormal realms. The journey began with other people. We were going to start filming our spiritual experiences and help others through their spirit difficulties or paranormal encounters. With all that I've seen and experienced, I wanted to help people change their lives for the better so they wouldn't have negative experiences and influences directing their lives. I know it's easier than one may think, but it takes work and dedication. I can't honestly explain how it feels when you see the negative energies surrounding someone. I do know you feel compelled to help them when you have the key to do so. When you can see negative energy, you naturally want to know why and attempt to understand this realm.

It's not just the physical world that needs help. The spirit world needs it too. Delivering messages and guiding the spirit world into the light or crossing a spirit over is something I do on many occasions. It can be difficult work to do and is done through prayer. If you're not a master of your craft, don't even attempt trying to cross a soul into the afterlife. Until you understand why they're here and what they need to accomplish in this physical world, they'll never leave, not until their work in this world is finished.

Human society has no power over the spirit world as this has no control of the physical world. Only God can make changes. This is a hard lesson to learn because the ego within us desires power and accomplishment. However, you do have control over your own life so in reality, no one can cross over a spirit at the flip of a hat.

I have a YouTube channel called Tea Time with Medium Marnie Hill. This is where I answer questions on my channel from people who email me questions regarding the afterlife, angels, life after death, or have spiritual questions. One day I was getting ready to do a talk about ghosts and negative attachments, this was to be a Halloween special. However, this episode on my channel tea time never took place. While I was speaking, the camera was rolling and two light bulbs popped! The lights in the room began to flicker, I became uncomfortable, and the person with the camera said that the topic was perhaps one that we shouldn't be talking about at that time. I agreed. Something was happening and I needed to listen. What I heard was it wasn't the right time for this conversation and that might have been because it was almost Halloween. Ghosts and evil don't just exist around Halloween and I think we've made a mockery of the reality of evil, so it gets pissed. It's not always evil or the spirit world interrupting electricity or causing some type of earthly activity. Angels can and will do it too, if they need to get your attention. So always pay attention to your surroundings and please don't look for a demon under every rock. You may find something else that may surprise you.

During my time in the paranormal world, I visited a local house that was presumed to be haunted. I was accompanied by my investigative partner at the time who had been a paranormal investigator for years. We were doing a Halloween special for a local television station. As soon as I stepped onto the front lawn, an older gentleman came to greet us. I could feel and see him for he was in the spirit realm, breaking through to this realm. I was to learn later that this gentleman was the former owner of the house and he was welcoming us into his home from the spirit realm. It was such a beautiful location. We went into an area that was closed to the general public. When I entered into one room, I felt nauseated and felt some negative energy upstairs. My partner was busy taking photographs to see if he could catch anything and he did! He took a picture of an orb in the same area of the room where I'd felt nauseated. My body was reacting to the energies within that location. I'm pretty sure the spirit wasn't right and there was also lots of residual spirit energy in the area. Residual spirit energy is old energy that has memories. Some of these sit within the walls, on the floors, and even on objects. This spirit energy eventually manifests to a more negative energy state if fed by fear or by negative thoughts or intentions.

That same week we were to visit a local restaurant. This location also seemed to be well known as haunted. In this place I was to use my ability as a medium. I was to speak with the spiritual realms or to any spirit that decided they wanted to speak to me. I wasn't there to investigate, I just needed to talk to the deceased. It was exciting for me. I had no idea if it would be the same as my house walkthroughs or similar to my in person or group readings. When I do a walkthrough, I walk through a location and read the spirit energy of the home or the general environment. I'm also conducting a clearing and blessing at the same time, so I set the intention for spirit to come forward. On this day, I set the same plan for spirit to come forward and had to be open regarding what I needed to experience, to help another soul. It worked because lots of things started to happen during my time at the restaurant. As soon as I arrived, I saw a spirit man and he told me he was the caretaker of the land. When I went into the bathroom and was washing my hands, a man came to the left of my ear and said hello then disappeared. Needless to say, I was startled. I could feel different spirit energy everywhere and the souls in the afterlife seemed to be more than happy to speak that day. I didn't know until that day that the restaurant had previously been a funeral home. A unique individual was trying to get my attention in the area where no one was allowed to enter but us. He was a spirit passer through, something that doesn't belong to the location. They can see my light and he decided to communicate with me. He was interested in what was going on. He'd passed away a couple of streets from the restaurant due to a drug overdose. He was stuck and didn't want to go to the light, so he hung around locations close to where he used to visit, where the drugs or his old friends were. He was harmless yet seemed to continually drain the energy from both our cell phones that day. When I spoke with a living individual at the location, a dog ran through the area, or rather a spirit dog. Then a man came forward from the spirit realm. I knew a message was being brought forward to the person that I was speaking with. I found out later that it was his friend that had passed. Through me, his deceased friend was telling him that he was with his deceased dog, taking care of him. This is exactly what this person needed to hear that day. You see, when I'm open spirit knows I will communicate with them and what needs to be delivered as a message will be delivered.

This type of communication can drain a physical medium such as myself. Randomly opening myself up to all sorts of energies at one time isn't easy on my soul or energy field. I would often ask myself why this is so draining if these souls are in heaven. In this line of work, you're dealing with dead energy that needs to transform to a different energy source when speaking and spirit uses my power to do it.

As an empath, everything you feel, see, hear, and experience is magnified when you're a medium. And this isn't something many people understand and neither did I at first. However, as I ventured on my quest I realized that my empathic sensitive skills were crucial to my ability to talk to the deceased.

During my time researching and understanding the ghostly realm, I began to experience what I was learning about and this wasn't my mind playing tricks on me. I can see the dead so naturally I can also see negative energy, evil, and even demons. By researching it, on some level I was permitting myself to experience it. I firmly believe that what you seek, you will find, your attention becomes your intention, and from that you'll create your experiences, whether you desire them or not. Even though I felt I was helping people, I began to feel a strange sort of numbness within my soul. Dark energy can do that to even the brightest soul and remember the devil wants your soul. I didn't like this feeling at all. When I work within the paranormal I protect myself differently than I do in my general medium readings. I still use rosaries and prayer, but it's different.

One afternoon, while away for the weekend, I was trying to have a nap but failed to fall asleep, which isn't unusual for me. However, as I was trying to relax and drift off to sleep, I kept feeling a little off energetically. I could sense something wasn't right within my environment. I tell people that my spidey senses were tingling. I sat up in bed, looked toward the wall and then I saw them, two entities standing near the foot of the bed. They had an evil look about them. The one that was closest to me looked directly at me. His eyes were dark, his skin was graying, and he looked a little like an ancient vampire, the ones you see in old movies. His nails were long and looked exactly like snakeskin. The other male standing near him had dark brown hair, black eyes, and similar fragile, pale skin and seemed to be glaring at me with a mean evil look.

"In the name of Jesus Christ and the power within our Lord, I command you to leave now," I declared.

They did leave, but not before the one resembling a vampire looked right at me. I knew demons were real, but this was way too close for comfort. At that moment, I wondered if a demon was haunting. Why was he trying to get my attention? Then I began to wonder if the location was haunted. I've had that experience before, just not as intense. As a medium, I see everything in the spirit world. There was a war going on in the unseen world. I could feel it. It seemed like I got evil's attention at some point and that wasn't a good thing. Evil doesn't like me. I shine too brightly for them. Thank goodness for my previous experience, knowledge, and my trust in Jesus. I went into prayer and I saw Jesus and Mother Mary and I heard them say that I was safe there. I was safe with Him in my life. The demons left as quickly as they'd arrived. I know my will is reliable, but God's will is stronger. There is and always will be a spiritual war going in the spiritual realms. There's no getting away from it. You may not be able to see it, but you can sense it. No matter how well trained you are or how good you are at protecting yourself, the paranormal or communicating with random ghosts is dangerous yet essential and much needed work.

This is work that I continue to do today. I now put restrictions on myself to protect my soul and the light that is within me. When I stay close to Jesus and keep my eye on Him, nothing seems to interfere with my life. I feel calm and at peace even when doing readings, spirit investigations, or house clearing and blessings. Evil doesn't affect me anymore. I've never had a demon, evil spirit, or wicked soul enter into my private or group readings. They seem to disappear when people are working one on one with me. However, they can't hide when I set the intention to speak to them.

My readings feel holy to me and all souls that are in heaven are coming from a holy place. Remember, there are different dimensions and levels within the afterlife. You can tap into many if you so desire but be forewarned that you might not like what you find. Please don't fall into the trap of what some people think or say about experiencing evil. It seems you can only believe what you've experienced and believe me I'm not the only one. I'm just a person that has the nerve to talk about it publicly. Just because someone hasn't experienced doesn't mean it isn't real. It also doesn't mean there's something wrong with you if you've experienced it. I help people with spiritual discernment, oppression, and with attachments. This is what I do.

It isn't unusual for me to have coaching clients or people coming in for a reading that are experiencing spiritual oppression. I was dealing with a client and she was deeply into occult practice and tarot cards. She used tarot cards every day. She used the pendulum, which is a divination tool, and meditation way too much, up to three hours a day! That's not living and if you ask me, she wasn't well. Not only was she suffering from grief, as she'd recently lost her daughter, but her energy was so low. She didn't even have the power to cry. She just slept and then tried to connect with her deceased loved ones and tried everything. After no luck, she came to me for a reading and coaching session. We connected with her deceased loved ones and they told me they were worried about her depression. She confirmed she had clinical depression, was seeing a psychiatrist, and was feeling unwell. I was also told to ask her to stop using divination tools. She confirmed she did but that she didn't want to stop. I mentioned Jesus and that I wanted to enter into a prayer for her. Now this isn't something I usually do, but I felt compelled that day. When I asked her if we could do a prayer, her eyes went dull. There was no light within them and the dark energy around her was thick. The spirit energy near her didn't want to have her go into prayer with me but she finally agreed to do it. I ignored what I saw and felt and we entered into prayer for healing. Eventually, her energy changed. I saw this dark, murky substance disappear from her. I could see light within her eyes and around her physical body. I could feel negative energy was removed from her. I asked her how she felt.

"I don't know," she said. "Something feels different. I feel lighter. Not sure what you did, but thank you."

Of course, it wasn't me. I just facilitated a healing that spirit was already doing for her. It was becoming more and more evident that spirit was trying to show me something and also where they needed me.

What I've learned is that evil wants to dim your life, scare you, and try to make you become an unbeliever in God. Darkness does this by making you believe God isn't real and tells you that God doesn't want to help you and has disowned you. God can't take away our pain and it's not up to God to make sure everything in our life is perfect. I do believe everything that happens to us happens for a reason. Remember, human life is short. Our presence in heaven is eternal, so maybe He has a plan for you. He also doesn't stop death. That's not His job. God created free will and Satan has free will too. If you live your life in such a way so that you can call dark energy to you, are unkind to others, or want harm for others and yourself, you're opening doorways for evil to enter. But it doesn't stop there. Evil and dark energy can grow, feeding on you. If you feed it, it continues, but if you starve evil of negative energy, it seems to disappear from you. It may not entirely go from a location but if nothing feeds it, it can't survive, so eventually it leaves or dies. Sometimes things happen in our life that are good, bad, or that we simply can't explain.

One day I received an email from a woman wanting me to come to her location because they'd been experiencing lots of unusual occurrences. She felt as if ghosts haunted her home. When I entered the house I could feel her husband's mother nearby. I had to ask the deceased mom to hold off for a bit. I needed to get everything in order before I was to start communication with her. She did wait, but she wanted to talk and I could feel her excitement. She had exciting news, news that would give validation of her existence on the other side and prove she was watching over her family. Messages were delivered and I then began my walkthrough. When I reached one of the bedrooms, I knew someone was going through a drug withdrawal or had recently experienced an addiction. The woman confirmed that this was their daughter's room and she was overcoming dependence on a very potent drug. I cleared the room, blessed it, and put holy symbols on the walls and above the door entrance. The energy in the room stay contained and spirit was working at releasing the negativity through me. Based on recent health issues with other people that were living in the location, if the energy moved it could have caused others to become sick too. Negative energy and evil also thrive on addiction to drugs of any sort, including excessive alcohol. I'm not saying everyone that has a drug addiction has an attached demon. However, I'm not going to say this isn't part of the problem because from what I've seen it could perhaps be a contributor. I will leave it there for now.

I find this next experience very interesting and a little scary too. Remember what I said earlier about how the soul heals when it enters heaven? During another reading, my client's sister came forward. She provided us with all sorts of validation and healing and wanted to speak. She then began to talk about something that made me feel a little uneasy yet intrigued at the same time. She'd committed suicide and began to share many messages with me, which my client confirmed as the truth. She told me she'd felt haunted in the physical world, as if demons were chasing her. I asked her sister if this is correct and she said that her sister had talked about it all the time. I then told the deceased sister, who told me that she was terrified of what she'd seen when alive and everyone thought she was crazy or suffering from schizophrenia. The client confirmed all of this. Then as I was talking to the deceased, she told me she wasn't ill, that demons had been following her and were real. She called them through by using spiritual tools and drugs she shouldn't have been using. This was just a little more confirmation for me.

Thank goodness they don't haunt me, but I can feel how painful this must be for one to endure and how needless it is too. Based on what she shared with me, her attachments caused her depression, which led her to take her own life. I feel society, not the family, failed her because of our fears and disbelief.

When I was in my early twenties, I was renting a basement suite from a woman. She had a boyfriend and I knew she was pregnant, although she didn't tell me this. I could sense a baby soul within and around her. She had had other pregnancies that unfortunately didn't make it to term. It seemed as if this one wasn't going to make it to the end of the pregnancy either, but I wasn't going to tell her that. One night while I was sleeping in the basement suite, I heard the voices of two young girls who sounded about four years old and then it felt like they sat on my bed. I sat up and yelled nicely for them to get out of there. They laughed and disappeared but this happened on several occasions. They told me they were sisters and lived in the house. One day I was talking to the woman and I asked if she'd had a miscarriage. She said yes and asked how I knew. I replied that

I just knew things and then asked her if she'd lost twin girls. She began to cry.

She asked me how I could possibly know this and I explained that they showed up to say hello and were having fun playing in heaven with each other and were happy. That was when the communication finally stopped with them. I delivered the messages and then I could finally get some sleep. Some of the ways in which the spirit world communicates with us can seem alarming and scary, but many times our loved ones are just trying to get our attention, to say hello. I always tell people that if they think their loved ones are trying to say hello they should say hello back. They should tell them that they feel their presence and talk to them. They could even write a letter about how they're feeling and leave it out in the open for the loved ones to see, perhaps beside the bed or on the kitchen table. It should be a place that is easy for them to find. This is healing for you and also healing for them.

My research took me on a spiritual quest, a religious journey to find answers regarding my abilities, life after death, and demons. I was being led by spirit to look into theology, listen to different speakers, ministers, and to read the Bible. I found it very disturbing that some people are convinced that mediumship is the work of demons and was something evil because the Bible said so. I often wonder who put that in the Bible, which has been touched by human hands, by rational thought, and by the human soul. What I've found is that there is insufficient evidence to back up the claim that mediums are connected to evil. Jesus didn't have enough time in this physical world to honestly explain the doings of the human world and the truth about His teachings.

I know some people become furious when others try and interpret the Bible, but as a human being, I have the right to ask questions when someone's calling me a demon or saying that the work I do is of the devil. This is spiritual discrimination all the way and discrimination of any kind is not the work of God. I'm here to help this world heal and if talking to the deceased or ridding someone's life of demons is part of it, then so be it. No one can ever try and tell me I'm not doing God's work, because I know I am. I was born with this gift. I'm proud to be a medium, not only a follower and a lover of Jesus, but a person that desires to help our world understand Jesus' love and truth.

So, what is negative energy? The best way to explain is that it's energy created by negative thought. You can feel this in an environment or around objects used for evil or harmful purposes. You can also sense this in a personal energy field. It's that hazy gray mist around people that are in the negative victim frame within their life. Many years ago, I was working with a client, coaching her with my Soul Enhancement ™life coaching program. My client had many years of trauma that she carried around within her life. As a spiritual coach, I was guiding her to release these thoughts by using gratitude and looking at her life differently. One day she was releasing some old anger and as she was speaking, I saw a dark black substance begin to fly quickly out of her mouth and move directly into my direction. It was heading straight for me. This was dark, angry energy from her soul. It looked like black tar and even though it was an energy form, it was flying all over the place. I quickly guarded my own energy field and let her keep going, since this process was bringing her healing. Eventually, she calmed down and the black substance stopped emerging from her. However, I was utterly drained and after she left I realized that I needed to not only cleanse my house with sage but also myself and put prayer within the area. If I hadn't done that someone may have felt the energy, which would then turn into residual spirit energy. This type of energy can give people headaches and make them feel angry, leaving them with no understanding of why they are feeling so tired or grumpy. The spirit energy or the black substance could grow if fed by other negative energy. I know this sounds crazy, but it's true. But it can't take over your mind, as only evil can do that. I've also seen this substance inside the body and cancer looks similar to it when I do readings or a healing session with a person.

Obviously, I've seen and experienced evil, but what about the darkness that sits within our world? Yes, I've seen it within our physical world and I'm pretty sure you have too. I've often asked myself whether evil can affect our thoughts and have concluded that it can and does so for many people.

As often as possible, I wear a cross to remind me of Jesus' love and sacrifice, along with a Saint Benedict charm to ward off evil. No one's going to dim my light. Mine is from God and so is yours. Yet no necklace will work if you only half believe in God's love, so keep your vibes high and keep faith close to your heart.

Darkness is real within the human world too. I've had many encounters with people that seem evil, as I'm sure you have too. We all have. I'm not referring to attachments on people, possessions, or anything like that. I'm talking about negative energy that dwells in the minds and evil that resides in the soul of people in our society. I've found that it doesn't matter what profession or industry a person is in. There's evil within this world and this is within people.

I wanted to write about my personal encounters in this book. However, I realized that if I write in detail about my negative encounters, I'm keeping those experiences alive and I don't wish to do that. God knows and He will do what needs doing, all in good time. Remember that when you feel overwhelmed by mean, evil people.

You can turn on the T.V., listen to the news, and ponder how many people have done you wrong in order to realize just how evil this world can be, but there's beautiful light within it too. I found darkness within my industry, with clients and with others that call themselves psychics and mediums and this is disheartening. Yet they only have power over you if you let them have such dominion. That's the beauty of free will.

I understand why many downplay evil in certain spiritual and metaphysical industries and try to convince themselves that hell isn't real. They don't want people to fear what they do. And remember, not long ago people were burned to death or otherwise killed for being a healer or having the ability to talk to the dead. If you study this topic, you soon realize that people were confused in those eras, not to mention hungry for money, power, suffering from starvation, and living with undiagnosed mental disorders, which doesn't sound much different than today's world.

The way I see it, in the olden days it could take one king to change the minds of people, along with specific churches and doctrines. All it took was some hard cash and fear for things to change quickly. A book called the *Malleus Maleficarum*, usually translated as *Hammer of Witches* and considered to be a witch hunter's bible, was written in 1486 and explained how to identify and kill witches. The hammer of witches book was actively used for nearly two centuries and perhaps longer, what a dark time. In 2018 it became legal to call yourself a witch in Canada. Yes, it was illegal until just recently. In the witch-burning era, there was big money in finding a witch and you got paid well. Perhaps you had trouble feeding your family and you didn't like the family on the next farm, because their crops were growing better than yours or they were earning more money than you. Or maybe you liked your neighbour's wife instead of your own. Would you be willing to tell the authorities what you suspected or desired to be so, for some money? Many people did this kind of thing back then, which is sad when you think about it. Now don't get me wrong I'm not a witch and nor will I ever call myself one. However, during my research on mediumship I was surprised to find how many people actually categorize mediumship as either the work of witches or the work of demons. I have no idea how a beautiful gift that can help so many people can be turned into something so dark and negative. It hurts my soul when I see the effect this evil thought has on our society.

Remember, I'm a truth seeker. I needed to learn all about the unseen world. As painful as it was for me to learn about the past and how misinformed we have been, I do still have faith in humanity. One day, or in one century, we'll understand and see the real value of truth.

Getting rid of evil and negative attachments

The best way I can help you is to recommend increasing your vibration or energy field, which is easier than you might think.

Remember what I said earlier, that your thoughts create your reality, so be mindful of your dreams and think positively. I try to find two things to be grateful for every day and thank God for them. In the morning, I thank God for my awakening and being able to shine my light for one more day. At night, I thank God for the day, the lessons learned, and promise to be an even better person tomorrow. Prayer is essential too. Prayer isn't asking for something and is more like having a friendly conversation with God. Although our purpose in life is to be of service to humanity, this means in service to God. When I pray, I ask God to show me the way and to give me a sign regarding what to do if for some reason I can't hear him within my prayers, asking that I might still receive signs or signals that He's listening. God and His angels work through other circumstances. It would be great if you had a direct telephone line to Him. That's the nature of prayer but it's very different to speaking with someone on the phone. God can hear you, but you should never demand things and simply have a friendly talk. I've also learned that God and His angels can hear your thoughts, whereas evil cannot, since it doesn't have that kind of power over you.

Watch what you put into your body and eat high vibrational foods. These include humanely raised animals and animal bi-products, organic vegetables and organic fruit. Stay away from street drugs and drink minimal alcohol. Be in service to others. At least once, hopefully more, do something beautiful for someone every day. Perhaps you can open the door for someone else, graciously smile or say good morning to someone you don't know, or donate to a worthy cause. In essence, you do good within our world.

Make forgiveness a priority. First, learn to forgive yourself for your shortcomings then you can forgive others too. Maybe you don't want to forgive them directly and this is okay. You can write a forgiveness letter, which will always show your life lessons and you can learn how to forgive without holding anger. I always tell people that when they're mad at someone, and your body is reacting to it for years, you're only hurting yourself.

Have a crucifix or items of high vibration near to you. Pictures of Jesus or angel ornaments will always raise your energy vibration. If you want to use gemstones within your environment or wear them, that's great too. Clear quartz, rose quartz, black obsidian, black tourmaline and hematite are excellent stones for that. Read the Bible and call upon Jesus when you feel uncomfortable within your space, but you must genuinely believe in Him if you want it to work. Listen to high vibrational music. Sorry, some hard rock doesn't work well for that. Minimize watching horror shows or avoid keeping items around your location that could look demonic to the naked eye. Stay away from Ouija boards, tarot cards, and negative people. Learn to use white light protection and clearing for your aura field. White sage is excellent for this. Most importantly, don't give your power away to fear or evil. Learn to stand your ground within this life and honour your own life. Wear high vibrational colours like the colours of the rainbow. Purple, blue, white, and yellow are good colours. And most importantly remember when we accept the self, we honour the Holy Mother and Father in heaven. Remember, this life isn't all about you, it's about all of us. There has been too much teaching of the 'self' instead of the 'us'. When you raise your vibration, energy attachments, entities or negative energy, will have a hard time sticking around you. Remember, you are in control.

CHAPTER SEVEN

~

Animals In Heaven

I am a lover of animals, mostly dogs, but I do love all animals. They seem to be unique and all of them have their personalities. Animals have a soul too. Believe it or not, animals go directly to heaven and I've never seen or been told that animals reincarnate into humans and humans don't reincarnate into animals. Their soul and their purpose are much different than ours. They're a part of you, when animals choose you. Just like the human soul, we pick the souls we want as our family. We choose the people we need in our lives to further the growth of our souls.

Every animal goes to heaven and they find their family, but they don't need to have to initially meet immediate family members. A dog may pass but if there's only a great grandparent from the family in heaven, the dog will be met by them. But animals are also creatures from God. They belong to Him and on numerous occasions I've been shown what animals do in the afterlife.

One day a woman visited me for a medium reading. As I sat down and began to prepare for our session, no human soul came through. I was a little perplexed at first.

"The only soul I have coming through is a dog. He's black, looks like a male lab," I said. "Does this sound like an animal that was close to you?"

The woman began to cry. She'd recently lost her dog and had come in specifically to talk to him. I was truthful and told her that her dog was here and willing to speak with me, but I also informed her that I'd never previously spent a full fifty minutes talking with an animal. To my surprise, we spent an hour talking to her dog. He showed me what he looked like, his passing, and his personality came through so strongly. He was a character. We both laughed at how he looked at life and his owner or Earth mother. He'd certainly been the man of the house. She had to put him to sleep because he had cancer. He told us he knew that and was okay with it. He even showed me where the tumour had been. I enjoy talking to animals in heaven. They still love their family, even from the other side.

In another reading, I had a young girl that came through. She was my client's daughter and after we went through all the validation of who she was and how she'd passed, she showed me a robin. She then showed me images of her painting birds, including a robin. Then several birds started to come through the reading and she asked me to convey to her mom that she was caring for animals on the other side, just like she would have done when she was alive. Her mother received a tremendous amount of peace. She knew her daughter was doing what she loved, even in heaven. To know that her daughter was still close to animals, being creative and painting in the afterlife, and taking care of animals was a memory that would allow her to move through her grief a little differently than if she'd not been aware of this. This girl felt like an angel to me when I was speaking with her during the reading.

I was once doing a small group reading at a home location there must have been about fifteen people in the room. I never knew that the woman that hosted the reading had two dogs in her garage. They were quiet and had never even barked when I rang the doorbell. It wasn't until about halfway through my session that I heard the animals in her garage. I was speaking with a deceased loved one and suddenly a spirited horse showed up in the middle of the room, so

I told the woman that her horse arrived. As soon as that happened, the dogs in the garage began to bark, really loudly and aggressively. It sounded as if they were going crazy. I was startled, not knowing at first if I'd heard dogs in the spirit world or the physical world. I was so shocked. I laughed and so did everyone else. Well, in essence, the dogs had sensed the other animal spirits coming from heaven. Animals can sense their loved ones in the room or even other souls that come forward, including other animals.

I've learned over the years that the personality of the animal never changes in the spirit world, just like the human personality never will. If the dog was stubborn, they show me this. The cutest dog I've ever spoken to was a fluffy female that showed me her beautiful pink collar. She told me that she'd been in dog shows and believe me she was pretty proud of her accomplishments. I saw how much she loved her family and how much they loved her. They like to paint pictures of their lives, just like the human souls do, it just comes through a little differently than it does with the human soul.

I've seen birds, cats, dogs, horses, and reptiles, in heaven but no insects, thank goodness. Animals can sense other animals in the spirit world. Your human world animal will do some things in the presence of a spirit or a loved one that has crossed over. A dog might stare at the wall where there's nothing and wag their tail. They may watch something in the room and their eyes seem to follow an image that others are unable to see. They may bark at nothing in the corner of the room or they might start acting very unusual for no apparent reason. If your dog is growling and seems very agitated or angry, there may be an evil spirit present within your location. I love animals and believe that they're sent from heaven to help us. They are family members too.

When we decided to have a dog enter into our world, we wanted to choose wisely, so we figured out the breed we would like and began our search. I never found anything in the city where I lived so I made an appointment with a breeder that lived a couple of hours away to see a dog. Then my husband called and told me that he'd found a closer breeder and we could all go in the evening to see the puppies. We were all excited and ready to go. When we arrived at the home, the breeder opened the front door then she took us into a room where the puppies were. They were all hiding, except for one. The woman looked confused.

"This is strange. I have three other ones and they seem to be hiding right now and the one that's come out to see you is usually the one hiding."

This didn't surprise me at all. We sat down on the floor and this little puppy came running! He was all over us, as if we'd just came back from a long holiday. We were all taking turns holding him and then the breeder found the other puppies but ours was unhappy about that. The male, his brother, walked by to check us out and our puppy barked as if to warn his sibling that we were now his. Our puppy never let any of the others come near us. We could see it in his eyes that he was ours. I told the woman that we'd take him, but that I needed to return in the morning with a kennel for the ride back. As we were leaving, he barked so loudly that it almost made us cry. We kept telling him that we'd be coming back for him and we did. He's now been with us for seven years and we've enjoyed every minute of his presence. However, he 's too sensitive to spirit and I have to put him into daycare when I do readings. He was at home with me for a while but he began barking right in the area where the souls would come through from heaven, using the door I'd created. People saw this as great validation and that a dog barking at thin air and acting like he was playing with a human was cute. However, it was a little distracting to me, to say the least, when my dog was actually interacting with the spirit world.

I've experienced some very unusual experiences when it comes to spirit animals. One day a woman emailed me to request a house blessing and a clearing for herself. She said she was sure there was something evil in her home and her husband was acting unusual too. I always exercise caution when people speak about feeling an evil presence that's affecting someone in their home. When I arrived at her location, before I rang the doorbell I could feel an immense spirit presence and also a lot of emotional pain before I entered the home. As I walked through the front door, I was shocked at how many animal spirits presented themselves to me. I felt a little nervous but didn't say anything right way. I began my session and after I left the living room, I told her I was picking up a lot of animal spirits, particularly a cougar, a bear, and other animals. The cougar wasn't a happy soul and I told her that his spirit was angry. The woman asked me to follow her downstairs and there were the animal heads, mounted on the wall. Her husband hunted animals for sport then stuffed them and these animals weren't happy at all. In fact, they were causing problems within the lives of the woman and her husband. The spirits of these animals were haunting the man that killed them, which was affecting the other family members. I had to do a family prayer and a clearing then had the husband do a prayer of forgiveness, so the spirit animals could move into the light if they chose to do so. I then taught him how to do another prayer after he made a kill if he was going to continue to take the lives of other animals, which he agreed to do. My understanding is that all is better within the home and within the family, for now. The lesson was learned that life isn't ours to take and if you do take an animal's life, you must receive forgiveness and thank it for its death. If not, the animals could try to haunt and hurt you.

Being able to communicate with animals in the spirit world has also allowed me to connect with the physical animal world intuitively, meaning that I can feel and sense what the animal is thinking. If you look hard enough, you can see smiles, frowns, unhappiness, and fear within their body language and within their eyes. I've found that animal energy vibrates quickly and I need them to slow their power down in order to speak with them, which isn't always easy to do, especially when my energy vibrates at a high level.

When the human world shows up in a reading, it seems that family members take precedence, meaning they speak to me first, before a friend would. However, pets seem to talk whenever their energy matches mine. It can happen at any time during the reading. They'll show me how they look and how they passed but it's so different, which makes sense since they're different to humans. Our pets go through a process after they're in heaven. They see how they passed away and the reasons why. I believe it's part of your guardian angel's job to do this. No animal is angry at their family for needing to put them down and the animal has an opportunity to understand. The saddest times for me are when an animal was lost and then passed away or was killed by another animal. Again, I feel their pain. It's nature. Animals are just like children to us within our world. They are a part of the family. Grief is grief, whether you lose a human person or an animal. It may vary in intensity as our relationships are very different, yet some are the same. I do encourage people to make sure they have some kind of memorial or something that's in memory of their animal. It can help you experience peace. Each time one of our fish passes, the children gather around, we do a little prayer, and off they go to fish heaven. I've never seen a fish in heaven. A bird yes, but not fish, although I've still never told my children that.

One time we had a fish stay with us for almost five years and he was getting pretty big. We remember him and miss him. Every time I did a reading, he'd go crazy in the fish tank. He had quite the personality and I had to remove him from the tank for a while because he was bullying some new fish and causing havoc. Yes, that was an exciting day, when he wanted to show who was boss.

I'm reminded daily how the deceased take care of their animals, the family pets in heaven, and that they enjoy doing this. Sometimes the deceased is an old family member and sometimes a close friend. I see animals being taken outside and visiting the locations where they loved to walk when they were alive. Everyone seems to take responsibility for souls in the afterlife. No one is alone, scared, abandoned, or needs to make their way on their own.

CHAPTER EIGHT

~

How The Spirit World Communicates

When the spirit world was talking with me as a child, I knew that I had to listen. I always had people in my room at night and I still do today. Sometimes I know who it is and on other occasions I wonder if they're passing through or are loved ones that I'll speak with soon. As a child, I had one particular elderly woman approach my bed and I screamed. My dad always came running into the room if I sounded scared. I told him who was in my bedroom and he had the strangest look on his face. He told me that there was no way she'd been in your room. The name I gave him was of a deceased great-grandmother and he explained that she'd passed. However, I never met her and I don't remember anyone talking about her. I was only five and my babysitter later told me this story, how I had deceased family members visiting me at night in my room and I would awaken screaming and my father would come in and see if I was okay. She remembers my dad speaking with her about it and how he found it all very strange. One man in particular scared me the most. He was never in my room and was always by the window, knocking and trying to get in. I could hear him as clear as day.

"Marnie let me in, I need to tell you something."

He had dark hair, was wearing a suit, and always had a carnation tucked in his top pocket. It would be many years later when my aunt showed me an old picture of our ancestors. I pointed to the dark-haired man in the photograph. I said that he looked familiar but she told me that he had passed ages ago and that I'd never met him. Well, I think you know where I'm going with this. I might forget names, but I never forget a face. He was the man that had talked to me when I was only five. That was around the same time that deceased family members were visiting me during the night to say hello.

One day my husband and I went for a walk and were talking about people that had passed away. It was coming up to the first anniversary of his mother's death. When I got home, I noticed a large white feather sitting on the chair at the end of my bed. I called my husband upstairs and he asked where I'd got the feather. I told him that I'd found it right there on the chair. We looked at each other and I told him that it was from his mom. She knew we were talking to her and this was her way of saying hello. All the windows were closed in the bedroom. I had no clothing or pillows that would have contained a white feather that large or indeed any feathers. It was a sign from above. My mother-in-law also tried to get our attention on another occasion after she passed away. One weekend we went camping in honour of her. On this trip we almost had a head-on collision but it didn't happen because something or someone told me to look left. My husband was driving and didn't see the truck that was heading for us. As we were about to turn, it came out of nowhere. My quick response caused my husband to quickly stop the vehicle, allowing us to avoid a collision. That same weekend as we were getting ready to pack up, I felt a presence. I had a suitcase with me because we were staying in a trapper's tent and cots were already set up for us, there was no need for a backpack. Everyone was out of the tent and as I was looking to make sure everyone had packed everything, when I felt a cold breeze behind my back. I turned my head, and looked directly at my suitcase which was laying horizontally and the top pocket which was unzipped was opened. What was in that opening, inside the top pocket may surprise you, as it certainly surprised me. I have three Lego parts, all standing symmetrically in a row. One was an Indigenous figurine, another was a dog, and then there was an arrow that the Lego Indigenous figurine was supposed to hold in his hand. They were all facing me inside the top pocket of my suitcase. I can't even imagine how they got that way or even in there. However, this suitcase had previously belonged to my mother-in-law. I quickly called everyone in and asked if one of them was responsible. They said that they'd been outside the whole time, but then my younger son spoke.

"Hey, I was wondering where these Lego figures went. Last time I saw the Lego was at Grandma's house!"

One day when I was driving in the car while going through some difficult times, I saw my deceased father sitting in the back seat. Naturally I was a little shocked. My deceased loved ones usually don't show up to say hello. Sometimes they do, but this is rare, although such visits are even more precious now that I'm delivering messages from the other side. My father telepathically told me to get a specific CD and said that this music would calm my soul and the words would help me with my troubles. Sure enough, I stopped off at the mall, got the CD, and felt completely at ease with the music.

Our loved ones know when we need guidance and are more than willing to offer a little help from time to time. Remember, there is free will. They don't have to provide support if they don't want to, but I've found most do. They are careful because they're in heaven and no one wants to stay in the in-between too much. There are other souls, good ones and bad ones, that move around within that area of the In-between.

Another thing I want to mention is that your family gets to know other family members and even your spouse's family gets to know your family members. When your loved ones are checking in on you during real-time they are going to see other souls too, souls that belong to you that are also checking in on you. Heaven is a friendly place and family is family. No one's considered a stepfather, mother, sister, brother, daughter, or son. They're family, so I never hear the word stepchild, for example. As for hearing, yes I do experience the spirit world audibly. This doesn't happen all the time, but sometimes it does. I seem to feel the presence of my dad, yet hear the presence of my mom. I can always hear her in my right ear. I have seen both my parents in the physical form from the spirit world, but this doesn't happen all time. Many people think that because I'm a medium I can speak with my own deceased relatives. However, this isn't the case. My abilities are used for others, not so much for me. That's the path of a natural born medium.

When one is sick, staying in the physical world can be a challenge. Have you ever wondered why your loved ones decided to pass away just after you left the hospital or decided to get a coffee? Well sometimes, based on what I hear, it's your energy and your love that can keep them here longer, even though they're ready to go. They avoid seeing your pain and it's painful for them before they go. Most people don't want to pass away in front of their loved ones, so they wait until the angels come down and tell them their time has arrived and sometimes that means you may get an urge to leave, go to the bathroom, get a coffee, or maybe leave for a couple of hours. This is out of your hands. Your drive will be so strong that you'll go, since this is governed by one of God's angels.

No one ever leaves the Earth alone. You have loved ones with you and your angels that have been watching over you. They too want to ensure that a safe passage is brought forward to you for heaven, but remember, going to heaven is also a choice, one that they all eventually make one day. Sometimes, deceased loved ones show up a few days before a loved one is to pass. They're hanging around and are prepared at any moment to escort the soul into the afterlife. It's not unusual for critically ill people to talk about their loved ones or say they saw them. They're not hallucinating and really do see

91

their loved ones. The veil between the spirit realm and the physical realm becomes very thin when a passing is near.

Being a medium doesn't allow me to see an impending death any more than you can. I may see a glimpse of destruction around them and then know that transition is near. If someone is sick I might be told a time is close and they need to get their affairs in order. That may include learning to forgive the dying or going toward them and telling them how you love them and how you feel. Anything that brings peace to the dying is beneficial and encouraged from the afterlife. I don't receive dates and times of a passing and in no way, shape, or form is a loved one or an angel going to tell me how my client is going to die and when. That would never happen. Me knowing this is considered a violation of privacy and I may unknowingly interfere with personal life if I did tell them. Premonitions do happen and mean that change is already in motion. You're not receiving an omen to change something. God would never require that of you or need you to do anything. But a knowing is a forewarning and sometimes that means get your stuff in order, someone is passing soon. Tell them you love them, mend old pains, as soon as possible.

Your loved ones may use another person to deliver a message, like the father who knowingly wanted me to talk to his brother. Have you ever been waiting in a line and earlier had some questions on your mind then hear the person next to you giving advice to someone regarding that exact topic? Well, that's your angels or loved ones guiding you at that time. They do this because they may not be able to talk to you, so they guide you to places and people that they can speak through.

I remember one day I was concerned about something in my life and my client answered the questions I was seeking. However, she had no idea what was happening.

"I'm not sure why I feel so compelled to say this," she said. "I read your first book and what you've been through, your experiences, and your pain. You should be really proud of where you are, what you've done with your life, and how many people you have helped."

I thanked her and wanted to give her a big hug. When she left, I sat down and no other words were needed. She provided the answers for me. God knows what you need and so does spirit.

Dreams are also a common method by which your loved ones connect with you. The best way to know if it's your imagination or a real loved one visiting is to remember that you'll feel your loved ones close beside you, so watch how you think. It may seem like your loved one is sitting across from you having a conversation within your dream. And believe me, their communications will be of importance. They won't be reminiscing with you, not in dreamland. Your loved one will also not make you feel fear and would never come through and be angry. Anger doesn't reside within the realms of heaven, only if they're stuck in the in-between or are in fact at a nasty level. If your loved one is angry the most probable reason is that your unconscious mind is trying to heal from something and is using your deceased loved one as a sounding board or a mirror, which is a reflection of your pain.

I often get questions about numbers. Do our loved ones communicate with numbers and coins? Yes, but this doesn't happen all the time and is rarer than one may think. I'm not saying it doesn't happen, but it takes a lot of energy to move items within the physical world from the spirit world. Unusual markings on the body may indicate that harmful or dark energy is doing this. It takes a lot of power and negative energy can create the kind of power that can move objects that cause infliction. I'm not really sure why but think it has something to do with anger.

I wonder where they would get the coins? I had one woman tell me that she saw a coin drop out of thin air and land on the ground. She was inside her house and no one else was around. She intuitively felt it was her dad and he confirmed this in a reading. What a beautiful thought and if you think your loved ones are leaving you coins, then keep that beautiful feeling. If you believe the angels are giving you coins, then this is okay too because maybe they are.

As for numbers, I do know that this communication is usually from your angels. However, your loved ones may telepathically send you a message to look at the clock, radio, or a sign you're passing or it may just be your guardian angel. The truth is no one knows. I say go with your intuition. If you think it's your loved one, then it is, and if you think it's your angel, then that's the case too. Please don't ask a medium to try and verify this in your reading. What if they missed the message, which would leave you thinking negative thoughts? Sometimes it's best to trust your intuition. Any loving message from your deceased loved ones or the spiritual realm is a gift. Try not to let the ego take over and make it into something else.

Your loved ones will also communicate or bring forward ways of communication that may be unique to you and them. There may be a particular flower they loved and you walk into a place and smell that flower when no flower is around. This indicates that your loved one is around. Smelling cigars or cigarette smoke may represent the same thing or it may merely be your unconscious remembering them and this smell brings them forward. If you find yourself thinking about your deceased loved one often, or at various times they seem to pop into your head for no reason, this is usually them too and your mind is picking up the image of their spirit as it's close to you.

However, if the spirit world needs to get your attention they will and will do this in all sorts of weird and wonderful ways.

I remember one evening I was getting a little angry at some of my family members, okay a little disappointed, and began raising my voice. The fire alarms then went off in my house, all two of them, and they were a level away from where I was. I thought it was the batteries, but all was good. The alarms didn't stop until I started to calm down. I knew intuitively that it was my mom from the other side warning me to calm down. After all, it was her grandchildren I was yelling it. This is how the spirit world can get your attention if they need to, by using the electricity. However, my own empathic abilities can also trigger electrical interference, so I'm always careful regarding my actions.

To understand the human world, you must understand the invisible one too. The spirit world is here to help us with our living world. And God hears you too but be patient, since nothing happens overnight and God and His angels don't work within our time. Situations happen within our lives, whether good or bad. Life happens and this is called living and believe me, this destiny thing is genuine. Some things happen, no matter how hard you try to have them not happen. This is part of one's soul contract. My experiences, make me who I am. Your life experiences make you who you are. Each of us is unique and that's why life is so exciting and a little mysterious at times too.

There are a couple of things you can do that will help bring your deceased loved one close to you. Think positively about them. Write them a letter and keep it out on your nightstand so they can see it. Keep pictures of them on display that give you happy memories. Jewelry has an energy imprint on it. Take a piece of their jewellery, put it in your palm, and hold it close to your heart then say their name and tell them that you love them. Never ask them to bring forward a message or demand they show themselves to you. Remember, energy that demands from spirit is energy that destroys. It must come from a place of love and with no expectations, just hope. Your loved ones know what you need and remember the rules of heaven. They can't and will not interfere with your life or the lives of others that are within your family.

CHAPTER NINE

Suicide And Heaven

Suicide is a subject that is very close to my heart. My mother committed suicide when I was young and she was only 28. I struggled with it for years. You'd think being a medium would make such things more natural, but it doesn't. We all deal with grief differently and it impacts each of our lives negatively. No one's prepared for death or prepared to experience a death. We're not taught in school or life how to deal with death. I think this is because everyone has their own belief system and it's up to the family or family members to help children understand death. As we grow, we learn to see life and death differently. We learn from our experiences, pain, and triumphs.

One might think that they'll be okay and be able to handle the passing of a loved one easily, but things change. How are you going to know how to handle something if you haven't experienced it before? When a loved one takes their own life, many family members have a sense of shame, and misunderstand the reason of the passing. Some people within the family may feel that suicide should or could have been prevented at some point in a person's life, leaving one feeling disharmony and anger moving through the family. Can all deaths be prevented? From what I've seen, I'm unsure. I like to think that deaths can be prevented but life generally moves along as it should.

Souls have come forward and shown me their lives, their pain, and their darkness. Many felt they couldn't pull themselves out of their pain, within the life they were living and this is painful to feel as a medium.

Why is this painful? Firstly, because of the pain associated with it for the living and the deceased. Secondly, the healing that needs to take place is heavy on the soul, especially when it's to bring about peace and understanding. Thirdly, they're usually not on the highest level on the other side. Some are stuck in that place I call the in-between. No matter how someone has passed or at what level they sit within heaven, it seems everyone is accessible to talk to if this is going to bring some form of healing to the inquirer or to their extended family and friends.

There is a specific symbol and look to the soul's energy field that tells me they committed suicide. They then usually tell me during the reading how they took their own life. Readings can become interesting for me. As a physical medium, I never want to feel a shot to the head or the chest but I will feel the pain, just not as intense within those areas. I've learned to listen to what my body is feeling during a reading. I need silence during my sessions to do this. Loud noise or people eating, drinking, or chatting amongst themselves is more than a little distracting, resulting in me missing important information. We get confused with what we see on T.V. about mediumship and believe me, it's not always a party.

If the deceased was taking lots of drugs before they passed away, I might feel it or they may show me the substances that they took. Feeling the addiction will make me sick to my stomach and sometimes cause me to feel dizzy, so I try to avoid feeling intoxications. Almost every soul I've spoken to that has committed suicide, and I talk to many, have another spirit with them that doesn't identify themselves. I call them a soul guide. From my understanding, this spirit is within them until they reach another level of healing then they move on. This angel also comes forward to ensure that the deceased soul that committed suicide doesn't get too close to me or drain my energy field. My angels are watching out for me, doing what they can to help. However, they're limited in what they can do, just like us.

There's always a caution brought forward in a reading when I'm dealing with suicides. I can feel it and it's interesting. The soul guide that accompanied them before seems to disappear in a reading when the deceased have gone through a number of levels of healing. This tells me that after they heal one will eventually go to a better level within heaven. Yet this doesn't take place until the healing is completed and this could take many years to come into fruition, as again there is no timeline within heaven.

I've also found that spirit communication must be all about healing when talking with souls that have committed suicide. They genuinely want to share why they took their own lives, as this helps them heal. And when one can get themselves to a place of forgiveness, it helps you and them even more. There are many reasons why someone may take their own life and none of them are good and that's how heaven sees it too. As painful as life may be, one must realize they need to learn how to move forward within life as everything is changeable. What makes my job difficult in terms of this is perception. Of course, the living are going to view suicide differently than the deceased, as each has their own separate view of the passing. When it comes to mental health issues and intoxication when people take their own lives, there seems to be some forgiveness that's brought forward from heaven. I have heard from the deceased that this is called a 'soul in distress', which requires a different form of spiritual forgiveness. The soul still needs to go into a specific level of healing on the other side, but the energy and concentration is different from that experienced by the ones that wanted to die. They seemed to have tried to take their lives before or written suicide notes. As hard as it might be to hear or read these words, suicide is frowned upon. No matter how you take your own life or ask to die, this is not something the other side takes lightly. We have a responsability in this world to help everyone avoid this. I'm just delivering the message that was brought forward for me to give.

I was speaking to a deceased young woman in a reading that was overcoming the pain of her addiction when she was alive. She said that overcoming her addiction was so painful that unless she was locked away in an institution, unable to get out and under lock and key, she'd never have been able to kick her drug habit. The emotional and physical pain of her withdrawal was so intense that she never even cared whether she lived or died. All she wanted was the drug. She showed me the dark energy that surrounded her. I've seen this dark energy before in my readings. Souls I've talked to, whether they were users or suffering from a mental illness, always showed me this dark energy around them. This energy might be an attachment, but it may also just be their way of showing me the intensity of their pain. However, this energy is specific to suicides where addictions were involved. It appears to me that life seemed too painful and that pain created a barrier where even light of their soul could not emerge. Whose fault is that? No one's really. It's sad, but pain is in our human world.

A question I seem to be asked frequently is whether you go to hell if you take your own life. I can comfortably say there is a high probability you won't be seeing your deceased loved ones anytime soon if you do. You'll receive healing in the afterlife for your actions, but no one knows for sure.

I'm going to talk a little about sensitivity later in this book. I've also noticed another trend with my suicide readings. Many people with mental health issues have a high degree of sensitivity and this might resemble a mental health issue at first, if not taken care of properly. If sensitivity isn't correctly nurtured and watched over, it can quickly turn into a severe mental health issue that may result in suicide, from what I've seen in some of not all cases. At least this is what I've seen from the other side. Life can be painful at times and occasionally complicated for anyone but empaths and sensitives can carry this pain with them and it's very real.

Being sensitive is a little different than being an empath and there are different levels to this too. An empath can feel the pain of others, which is never fun. Yet you can learn to desensitize yourself a little. If you take care of your mental, emotional, and spiritual self you can live a reasonably healthy life. I've done this for years. The changes a sensitive must make have to be life changing, consistent, and involve a commitment to one's self forever. One of the areas on which I've learned to concentrate is the spiritual self. While I take care of the physical by watching what I eat, working out, and by eating high vibrational foods, I also found that engaging in daily meditation and prayer keeps my energies and mind grounded and in balance. It was the acceptance of Jesus into my life that helped my sensitivity and my spiritual self. Empaths and sensitives must gravitate towards firm vibrational beliefs to feel more at peace. Being cautious about my surroundings has been helpful. Negative people are very toxic to sensitives and empaths. This toxicity can overwhelm you, leaving you feeling negative and depressed. When my energy begins to feel low, I always do a self-check and see whether it's me that's feeling this way or if I'm picking something up from my surroundings. Heaven wants us to heal during our living life so we can concentrate on the eternal life that awaits each one of us. However, if you're busy healing in heaven, it seems one may be spending some hard times rehashing past painful experiences. Learn to live your living life with gratitude, forgiveness, and love if you want to keep yourself on your heavenly path. Heaven might be beautiful, but you don't want to get there before your time.

CHAPTER TEN

~

The In-Between

Throughout this book, I've mentioned a place called the in-between. A lot of spirits seem to reside within this area. The in-between is the area where I safely open a door that allows me to speak with deceased loved ones. As a medium, it was vital for me to create this door as it enables me to live my life now and this is important to me. I don't believe every medium needs to use a doorway, but I can say that it's helped me tremendously with my gift.

Even though your loved ones are close by, heaven doesn't reside on Earth. It's in another place, away from our energetic human world, and I do believe it's beautiful. Our loved ones must move through a barrier or a veil to speak with us and to reach us, they move through the in-between. Remember when I talked about an angel that seems to be with souls that have recently committed suicide? Well, this is because of the in-between. On some level, souls can decide not to go back to heaven, learn, and move towards God. The in-between is located between our world and the next. Within the in-between reside the good and the evil spirits. I do believe the in-between also has an entrance to hell to the lower level, but the door I created contains only love and light so no harmful spirits can come to me or my clients. This is important to me too and is why I choose to be the medium that I am. God knows about this door and so does the spirit world. Spirit knows who comes to see me way before I do. They know what's going on in our society and within our lives. But they aren't like us, as they aren't human anymore.

It isn't unusual for your loved one to come and visit you from heaven on the morning before your appointment with me or even a couple days prior. I had many clients tell me they sensed their loved one was with them before they came to see me. Believe me, they are and they tell me things.

From what I've seen, it's quicker to bring through a soul that has chosen not to go to heaven and is an evil spirit than it is to attract a kind one. This is because evil sits and waits for disruption and this is why you need to be careful when communicating with the other side.

Your loved ones are busy in heaven healing, living with God and preparing for your return. Think about it this way, that heaven is on top, the in-between is in the middle, and hell is below. Hell isn't a place I've ever seen. Once you enter hell, you can never go back to heaven, so there's no movement between realms, meaning that you can't be in hell and go to heaven overnight. You're either in heaven or you're in hell. You can visit the in-between for a while and then you must leave and go back to heaven. Can you go back to hell? I assume so, since that's how demons travel through the realms. I have no idea if a person can eventually reach heaven from hell after healing. No one has said anything to me about this topic from the spirit world, probably because I don't talk to demons. Your deceased loved ones don't know either and perhaps that's part of things that are on a 'need to know basis' on the other side.

I do know that hell is for demonic souls, the evil people that lived within our world. You can get into the in-between, as this seems to be the place of free will. The in-between is also the place where ghosts live and not all spirits are evil. Some are stuck and prefer not to go to heaven and this is their choice. So, they remain close to the human world, in the in-between. However, I do believe they're being persuaded to go to heaven by God's angels.

Our deceased loved ones don't act the same as us anymore and have no ego and no requirements to judge or cause pain or fear. Only the souls or spirits that aren't in heaven have this access or this desire. However, it's interesting that within the in-between your loved ones will have an opportunity to meet other loved ones that are watching over you. I know your loved ones will meet your friends and people you may have known before your loved ones passed and then went into heaven. I've received many strange looks when I tell a client that their dad or mom knows their best friend. My client usually points out that they never knew each other on Earth but I explain that things change once you reach heaven.

Before we end the first part of this book, I want to recap a couple of things that are important for you to remember moving forward. If your loved one is in heaven they will indeed follow what's required of them when providing information to the living. My spiritual team that I work with from the other side provided me with rules of communication that all should abide by. I'll only speak of a couple. I take my work as a medium, intuitive, and messenger very seriously. I know what awaits me on the other side.

Heavens rules for spirit communication:

> Never negatively impact the living.
> Never interfere with living life.
> Always speak the truth.
> Only provide what you know as truth.
> Never answer a question you feel uncomfortable answering.
> Never pry into other lives and then relay this information to the living.
> Never tell your loved one to do something, only guide them if need.
> Only share information that helps the soul grow.
> Remember free will.
> Remember your loved ones must never rely on you for answers.
> They must learn to move forward.

Only divulge to the living what the living needs.

In the next part of this book, I've written about the importance of healing and enhancing your soul. You need to protect your soul in this world and live a life that's pleasing to God. The Bible shows us some of the ways that are beneficial for you but try not to get confused by its words and then create anger or mistrust against it. People who choose to teach the Bible are trying to come from the right place, but they're also human. And they will make mistakes, as sin is in our nature.

There is a beautiful place called heaven and beautiful souls are there waiting for you to make the right decisions, to live the life you were given, and to help make this world a better place. If you want to do something for your deceased loved ones, then be this for them. Learn how to become a warrior for God or at least a warrior of peace.

Prayer for you

"May the power of God be greater than the power that sits within our world. May God soften your heart and bring light into your pain. May your soul become unafraid of the lessons of our world. Instead of turning into darkness, I hope you embrace the light and allow yourself to fall into the arms of His love. For then, creation within you will awaken and the desire to understand and believe becomes your quest for truth and love."

Marnie

CHAPTER ELEVEN

~

Regrets From The Dead

Free will is real and helps us grow. As humans, we have free will within our world and we have an ego that's part of our human form and part of free will. The ego sheds the body after we die and doesn't come with us to heaven. However, all must enter the in-between place to determine where they'll go after they pass. When free will comes in, the soul has the right not to enter the realms of heaven and instead remain as an astral body within the spirit realms of the in-between and have access to the physical energy realms of our world, leaving them with the worldly name ghosts. God can't take away the ego or the shadow self as this is what makes us human and allows us to learn, grow, and heal our soul. You must experience pain for the soul to grow, but you'll only grow when you finally learn how to love, even without forgiveness. You must let life unfold as it is, learn, and grow.

I've seen God do His work within a reading when we communicate with a deceased loved one and healing happens. But don't assume that God is present in every situation. I've seen from others that have had a reading with me say that they felt closer to God after a session and their reading reaffirmed that heaven is real and they desired to change their life accordingly. Now that makes me jump for joy!

Yes, let's listen to spirit. Even though the deceased spend time in heaven with other loved ones, their main focus is learning how to get closer to God. It would be nice if we learned how to get closer to God on Earth, other than waiting until we are in heaven. The dead have expressed regrets to me. They have this feeling in heaven, until they heal from their memory.

I was doing a reading for a young man that wanted to speak with his brother. His brother came through and he'd passed at midlife from a sudden illness. My client never had a chance to say goodbye to his brother as they lived in different provinces. My client was also in a different country when his brother passed away. He died within three months of being diagnosed with stomach cancer and my client needed to say goodbye, which he did through the reading. What I found interesting was that my client asked his brother if Jesus was with him. His brother told me that Jesus was here, but he hadn't seen him yet as he'd done something earlier in his life that he needed to heal from. He wouldn't elaborate and this is okay too. Perhaps the brother didn't know what he'd done and this couldn't validate it.

I don't want information coming through in a reading that can't be verified, unless there's a possibility that we can get verification at a later date. You see, his brother was on a path of healing in heaven and part of his healing involved saying goodbye to his brother, after which the next phase would present itself, when needed. This is a common theme from the deceased. When they talk with me, they're coming from a healthier mind and soul. Their life is different now in heaven. They can see their old ways and realize they were caught up in the presence of pain and some of the decisions they made while they were alive didn't matter until they reached heaven. Once they're there, perceptions change and they want to change their ways from when they were alive.

The deceased wish they'd have spent more time with family and friends and less time worrying about money or personal and professional status. When you go to heaven, you take you. All your possessions including your bank account, no longer matter. The deceased have told me that they're learning now about the importance of taking better care of themselves. The dead can see where they went wrong. Also, they understand the importance of living in the moment and realize that they shouldn't have spent so much time dwelling on the past. Instead of wasting time feeling angry, they'd have forgiven earlier and said more often that they loved someone, were proud of them, or that they accepted them as they are. The dead wish they would have made a mends with the people they hurt. Sometimes in life we don't realize the amount of pain we're inflicting on another person's experience, not until we die and have the opportunity to see their pain. I've seen how the dead need to relive and feel the pain of others that they've hurt. By relieving the pain, we learn how to heal it. The deceased wished that they'd listened more to their inner voice of love and stopped trying to please everyone and think negatively about themselves. In essence, they wanted to love more and hurt less, including enjoying themselves and the soul and body God gave them.

When God made his blueprint for the human body, he created many parts for us. He needed to do this so we could learn to live life with ambition, to move through the race of time. We have to learn to move through life with grace. Only then can we realize we are never alone. If you're reminded of painful moments with your loved ones, I want to share some advice with you. Let it go! Your loved ones can feel your pain and yet they can do nothing about it, which sounds a little hellish if you ask me. So how do we remove the pain? Find something to be grateful for regarding your loved one. Everyone in our life is a gift, and whether it's a gift of love or the gift of learning, one must learn so they can heal and move on.

One way to learn how to heal is to focus on gratitude. Make a list of ten things you're grateful for within your life and a list of ten things you can be thankful for regarding the person you've lost or a person that may have hurt you. Anger is essential to include in your thoughts as anger can be turned into a positive when looked through a positive lens. Pain is here to allow us to grow. If we can see the lesson of the pain then we can heal the pain.

Some might think, well, my father was a creep and I'm glad he's gone. I get it, you're mad, but your anger is going to a place that doesn't exist and the past has dead energy in it. If you focus too much on past pain, the power that's in you can't move to the present so it accumulates around you, creating negative energy. We always need to move forward. Negative energy is different from evil spirit energy, but if the negative is fed through harmful intentions long enough, it will turn into evil energy. This results in you feeling tired, angry, pessimistic, hateful, and generally not a happy person. Then the ego can take over and cause real havoc with your mental and physical health, slowly destroying your soul. You're the one keeping the pain alive by feeding it. When you make that gratitude list, look at the pain and declare that your anger has made me strong and that from your strength you've created a positive path. I've learned the importance of being a kind soul, so perhaps through your pain you desire to help another. How you consider this is how you will find the gift. Don't be negative and say that your dad was a creep, he caused a lot of pain in your life, and you can't accept the reality of that. Instead say that the pain you endured from your dad made you strong. You're a strong person because of the pain your dad put you through. I've learned to take that strength and pain and put it to good use. Because of this, my personal life has excelled. I've learned the value of true friendship with my children, I strive to be a good mom, and I show my family I love them. You could try saying something like this.

"I want my family to have the love that I never had and they will through my actions."

Then thank your father for the experience.

"I now free myself of the pain and forgive you, Dad. You no longer control my life, for I've turned my pain into a gift of love and from that, I'll forever be grateful."

You can switch the words around as needed, using mom, dad,

aunt, uncle, or the name of your friend. What I want you to see is that no matter what happens with your life, you have a choice regarding how you want to see it and what you want to do with your pain. You either give your power to another or you take it for yourself and use it for good. Your list is a gratitude list for you, so make sure you don't just look for the happy stuff. Look for the pain and see how it's made you into who you are today. And if you're not happy with yourself, then change it. Don't live as the victim. Becoming a survivor is the best thing you can do for you, your loved ones, loved ones in heaven, and your soul.

Now imagine that you lost a loved one but can't move through grief and you had a loving, beautiful relationship. Everyone is a gift within our life and not every gift can stay, but consider what we've gained from the gift within our lives. Put your positive memories of your loved one into your gratitude list. Memories of the past and your loved one are gifts, so be sure to cherish them. When you're feeling down or missing your loved one, pull out the gratitude list and thank them for being a part of your life. When your deceased loved ones see this, and they do, they'll be happier for it and so will you. Don't fall into the trap when people say that you need to move on, forget them, and live now. Some people think it's crazy when a person keeps honouring their loved ones passing, but I never think this. I grew up knowing my that my grandma was going to have a big dinner in celebration of my grandfather's passing. We were celebrating his life, a time to remember, but remembering should always be when you want it. You don't need to have a special day to honour your loved one's life. If you wish to acknowledge their presence, then live your life the best way you can, for you and for them. Sometimes it's painful to revisit memories, but one must remember that we have these memories so we can heal and value what life once was. I'll talk more about the gratitude list and forgiveness later on in the book, so hold onto your list. You'll need it.

CHAPTER TWELVE

The Presence Of Angels

Faith comes by understanding and hearing the word of God. Your faith in angels will increase once you experience their presence. Angels are mysterious for sure. Angels don't give us their names as a name is associated more with the ego that resides outside of the heavenly realms. If you've had the opportunity to meet your guardian angels or a spirit angel and you feel destined to call them a particular name, then by all means do so. I assure you that they'll not be offended. Angels work for God's will and I prefer to call them angels of the Lord. Our world has become fascinated with angels, which can be a good thing and a bad thing. Angels never want to be glorified and they want you to be closer to God than them. I mean when you think about it, God is their boss and due to free will, they don't want to upset Him. I believe they've learned from the past. Since angels work for God, they don't work for us, meaning that you should be careful how you approach questions to an angel. In reality they have more power than you. Each one of us has an angel watching over them, which I like to refer to as a guardian angel. They also don't provide names unless it's imperative to do so. I've seen that our loved ones not only greet us when it's our time to pass into heaven, but your guardian angel will take you through the bridge of time. This means that much of your life review will be done with your guardian angel too. I spoke about this earlier, but due to free will the deceased don't always want to cross over into the light right away. Consequently, their angel awaits with them as perhaps they have some unfinished business on Earth or want to wait around a bit until they've had a chance to see their funeral or their loved ones one more time from the spirit realm before going to the heavenly realms. If you're wondering what happens to evil people in this world, evil is a choice and the angels don't stick around. That's when a demon waits for their soul unless they become saved in one way or another. And angels don't intervene because of free will.

Now that I've had a chance over the years to understand the spiritual realm, I think it's important to note that spirit guides are angels. They're just at a different level from other angels. There are many names from a variety of different cultures regarding even the word 'spirit' but it was a while before I got the message through from them it's now 'angel' for me. And it's okay to call them a spirit guide, they won't mind. They want to help you get closer to God and heal within your human world. Angels are God's creation, created before Earth, and God is the one that created them and He can create as many as He wants. God can develop angels at any time and deceased loved ones never become one of God's angels or spirit guides. I know you may have heard otherwise and while it's nice to think this, it simply isn't so. Our soul needs to evolve to reach the place where angels reside. Can a deceased loved one eventually become a lower level angel? Yes, they can but they remain lower level. Higher level angels never need to have lived within the physical realm or to have endured the pain of our world. They see everything from the other side. Our loved ones look over us, check in to see how we're doing, and sometimes really take an interest in our lives when we're going through difficult times, but at no time are deceased above God's angels. There's so much misinformation about angels. I found that once I looked to scripture and asked the afterlife, they agreed with what's in the Bible. Now I'm not saying they told me everything because they won't do that. Perhaps because they too are on a 'need to know basis' just like us humans. When a deceased loved one moves up a level toward becoming a lower level angel, they're making their way up to God. They're learning to be one with God and they do this through healing. It could take many, many years for this to happen and I don't think it happens within our human lifetime.

I've had many good experiences with angels earlier in my life. As I investigate more about the unseen or spiritual realms, I seem to learn more. I do feel it's important to recap some of those previous experiences. So remember as we journey forward, it's important to remember that angels work for the will of God. Even though they're here to help us, they govern, oversee, and sometimes guide us only through the description of Gods will. It means they're holy and we must approach them in this way. When one is sacred, respect is required and expected.

Angels will use every opportunity they can to speak to us, to help us when we talk to them, but you could be talking to a deceased loved one and the angels will hear. For a couple of days, I was asking my angels for some guidance, but nothing was coming through and they were silent. One morning I asked again, but there was still nothing. As I was driving, I remembered I needed to get some cash from the bank. I went into my bank and after seeing the long line up, I decided to go to the machine, which I'd used many times before. I seemed to be waiting for quite a while for my cash to come out of the device. In fact, the machine was making a loud noise, so I thought perhaps it might not be working. One of the bank employees looked over at me and I called her over, explaining that for some reason, my money wasn't coming out of the machine. Then within a couple of seconds, the machine started working and the money came out!

"Oh my gosh," I said. "Now it comes out as you arrive."

She said that it must be my aura. We laughed and I remarked that her energy got things done then thanked her. As I got back into the car, the answer I was looking for was aura! This was the one word that would have answered my question, the question I was asking my angels. This was no coincidence. The angels needed this to happen and I got a message just at the right time from someone that I never even knew. Now if this is the only way they can break through the barrier of your mind and soul, then it's good. Angels know how to get things done!

From what I've seen, there's lots of stuff going on in the spiritual realm or unseen world. I've tried many spiritual tools to see if I could get answers from the angelic realms and not one of them worked properly for me. Listening to my intuition, my spiritual team on the other side through meditation, prayer, or looking for good signs have worked, but nothing else.

I used to teach the pendulum until I realized it works precisely like demons. It tells you what you desire and doesn't necessarily tell you the truth. It will tell you what you'll receive based on what it is you desire but nothing ever comes to fruition. If you haven't heard about the pendulum it works in the same way as dowsing for water did in the old days. It picks up a fast-moving vibration. If something is desired or is favourable to your needs, you'll receive a yes if the vibration is high. If the desire is harmful to your needs, your vibration is low and will give you a no answer. It feeds the ego and that means it feeds off the negative and positive vibrations you're creating through your desires. I can't tell you how many times people told me they asked the pendulum regarding other people. Please don't do this. And besides, it may not be accurate. This is also considered an invasion of privacy when asking questions about other people, including your loved ones. The light doesn't answer questions that invade privacy, ever.

I've tried the pendulum hundreds of times over the years and this is precisely how it works. It operates with your energy and your power can come from your thoughts and desires, even the unconscious ones you aren't aware of. Throughout time these thoughts and passion can change. This is why the answers vary and it gives you what you desire. Remember the magic mirror and the saying 'mirror, mirror on the wall who is the fairest of them all' in the story of Snow White and the seven dwarfs? The mirror tells what the questioner desires to bring positive vibrations to all, but these aren't positive and only seem that way at the time. It's also called spirit trickery. It can be very addicting for many. I've seen it with other people and it can also be hazardous. Your ego will take over the shadow self and you'll ask questions you shouldn't be asking, which in return will bring forward negative energy. When this happens, you're no longer in alignment with your soul truth and angels have a hard time getting through.

Since angels work for God, He sends His angels when one may need an intervention. I've had many experiences. One day while I was driving, I was intuitively told by my guardian angel to change lanes. Actually, I heard the request to change lanes in my right ear. No one was in the car with me. I was told to do this just before a truck dumped his rolls of insulation all over the road. I may have been hurt if I'd stayed within that lane on the freeway, but my guardian angel had my back. One evening I was told to go to a specific place at a particular time for me to see something happen, which was very important for me to see. My life altered as a result of this experience. Angels have been known to intervene in people's lives, saving them from death, and they've been known to show up in human form and disappear when a message is delivered.

In all of my searching, I couldn't find many names of angels or demons in the Bible, but there are many names of angels and demons in other books. I found that interesting. Some of the names people are giving angels and the act of putting an angel into every part of life is just strange and unwarranted and the same goes for demons.

I've read and listened to deliverance ministers talking about demons of finance, devils of relationships, and demons of self-infliction. It's just one demon and that demon can take care of all your afflictions if you let it. There are thousands of demons that walk this Earth, I'm sure of it. They've been here on this planet long before we arrived and they have no intention of leaving. They are the fallen angels and choose to work against God. They want all the glory and pain gives them glory for then they know that they have control. There's a balance within our universe and I hope there are more angels than demons within the unseen world. I think God knows what He's doing and makes angels frequently. Guess we won't know until it's our time.

I know I might be making some people uncomfortable with this topic with what I've learned over the years. If you want to have an angel come forward, then please either call upon Archangel Michael, or say 'I call upon the angels who are closest to God.' By saying these words, you'll bring forward angels that are of the pure light.

The more I learned about the Bible and Biblical times, the more questions I began to ask souls in the afterlife. I could then see the conflict with our world because the deceased loved ones told me we need to put God first, not the angels. I mentioned this earlier in the book. During a reading with a woman, a deceased loved one told me to stop thanking my angels after the reading and to thank God instead. She wasn't the only one that spoke of this within heaven either. Today, I put my faith and gratitude in God, Jesus, or the Holy Spirit. If you do have an angel or a spirit angel or spirit guide with you and they don't want you to go to the highest of all, they might instead insist or request that you go through them first. Then you know this isn't an angel of light with you. You have something else guiding you on your path and this isn't a good thing. If you're uncertain who is guiding you, request that Jesus come close to you. Follow Him and any attachments that shouldn't be with you will eventually fall away, although they won't leave without a fight.

Angels are here to help you and guide you on your path, so don't be afraid of them and respect them. They'll fight for you and for your soul and most of all remember that angels are always in disguise.

CHAPTER THIRTEEN

The Sensitive Soul

I started to ask a lot of questions some years ago regarding my sensitivity. My need and belief in prayer was so loud that I wanted to understand why I'm so sensitive and what it meant for me. I'm not the type of person that will say that this is me so live with it. No, that isn't good enough. It wasn't good enough because of the conflict that being sensitive was presenting itself to me. I was so sensitive, yet I was sensitive to God too. One day I thought it would be an excellent idea to start a prayer service with my company. I mean, you offer services within your company because you love to do them, right? However, evil began to step in. While I was offering prayers to others that needed them, Satan's door opened and his minions began to wreak havoc within the prayer system. Some of the prayer requests were evil. Asking God to hurt another person is the work of evil, I think, and so does heaven. Requesting riches isn't a reasonable prayer request. Then I realized that many in our wold don't know how to pray the way God wants us to pray. As much as I wanted to offer this service, I wasn't prepared for the backlash that doing this kind of work as a medium would bring. Then the conflict set in. I needed to do this work, so then I began a discreet prayer service that only Jesus and I knew about. Prayers were given freely when I saw the need and no one was the wiser but me. I didn't start a prayer service because I was looking for glorification or someone's approval. I was trying to fill a need. I have a YouTube channel where I talk about the afterlife and heaven. I always tried to end it with a God Bless. This felt natural to me. However, I got a message on my phone from a troubled young man saying that demon workers are not to say God Bless. This guy didn't even try to hide himself, for I had his phone number. I deleted the message but then received another email message shortly after that, saying something similar from a completely different person. Needless to say, this was also deleted. I'm good at deleting emails or phone messages when I see evil at work.

You'll notice that earlier in the book, I was speaking about being sensitive and an empath and quickly mentioned the gift of mercy. Well, this was also part of the quest to understand me. Like I've said before, so many people get lost with their sensitivity and think they should walk into the path of spiritualism, New Age, or occultism. This isn't the case and I believe it should be avoided at all cost whether you are a sensitive, empath, highly sensitive, hypersensitive person, or have the gift of mercy. God put this in you so you could do good in the world. However, our world is in torment and doesn't have enough information about this yet. Our world is still trying to understand intuitiveness, sensitivity, ESP, and spirit communication. If we add religion into the mix everything starts to fall apart. I'm talking more about the area in the Bible that says God doesn't love mediums, psychics and so on. This is what happens when people begin to get confused about religion, science, and the human condition. Again, all hell can break loose. God loves all but evil wants you to be confused and hate others.

Whether you're looking into the medical system, the new age movement, or just trying to understand your abilities you'll find something different within every area. In this book I'm merely stating some quick facts. Many people, including myself, that were born with a level of strong abilities, view life differently, feel differently, have different energy, and have unusual experiences as they sense the world differently. There's nothing fun about being sensitive, yet many people try and tell others that sensitivity is simply a doorway to further your spiritual abilities. In truth, it's a gift and what I discovered through my research is you can call it many things depending on the industry you are in, yet they are all so similar.

We can see how industries adapt to their belief systems when each is more categorized together. People will move towards what their belief system is, holding it as truth, yet they all mean the same thing. I've learned sensitivity, empathy, and intuition can also be called a spiritual gift of mercy. There are some similar characteristics to all four separate areas and separate qualities to each gift, namely the gift of sensitivity, the gift of being an empath, the gift of intuition, and the gift of mercy. Even though we're all different, each person has been explicitly designed under the unique workmanship of the creator, God. What if I told you that you have these abilities because God wanted you to have them. The gifts He has given you make you who you are and if you use them wisely you may change your life for the better and help another while on your own path, in a way that allows the creation of our world. Our world is in pain and we need sensitive, intuitive, and empathic people that hold the gift of spiritual mercy to better our world. You'll see that there are only slight differences with each gift, but the real gift is the one that God desires for you.

I'm here to tell you to please embrace your gifts, help God with his mission on this earth, and don't expect anything in return except peace and happiness. You never know, your words of kindness, your beautiful smile, your sincerity, and the desire to help another might save a person's life, including your own. My conclusion is that whether you're a sensitive, intuitive, empath, or have the gift of mercy, this is a human condition with a fundamental spiritual aspect if you choose to see it that way. I've also concluded that many of these conditions, if not dealt appropriately for the specific individual or soul, could turn into a health condition or mental health disorder when it doesn't need to. We should be cautious when moving forward and understanding our own unique personal self or situation. Everything in life is energy, including your soul

The soul is unique to you and I don't believe it's either male or female. It just is. If you identified as male in the physical world, you come through as male from the other side in a reading. If you identify as female, you come through as a female. If you're both, something is usually said to me regarding identification, but not always. It's the soul that matters to the afterlife, not your sexual orientation. I can feel the male and female energy within the reading. Our energy system is what projects our beliefs and desires and our soul projects us as us. I've learned to trust the energy pattern of the soul. The energy encompasses the mind, the body, and the spirit, which when combined makes the soul. The soul is what we take into the heaven. I've met lots of people that are gay, bisexual, or transgender, and many of them have the energy system that they prefer to identify with. This means that I can feel how they define themselves, even without seeing them as it's an energy pattern. If it's an energy pattern of the soul, this is something that can't be changed nor should it be unless the person desires this.

When we try to be something we're not, our soul becomes in conflict, which can cause all sorts of problems. I've had many people in readings ask their loved ones if they're okay with their gender identity and to be honest, a comment comes directly from your loved ones before the question is even asked. Your deceased loved ones know what you need. Not one soul from the spirit world has come through with anger or judgements, because it's not the soul that judges but the mind of the human world that judges before one enters into heaven. Life is a gift that God has chosen to give in all its perfect and imperfections. We must have faith that God knows what He's doing and trust that the only response is respect and love. A person can relate to other genders or identities and still be a believer and a good person. It's painful when I see hate crimes and as a psychic and a medium I've felt it too. Maybe not as intense as others, such as gender identity that is now coming to light, but I can imagine how fearful one must be 'coming out' when we're still trying to understand religion, the human body, the soul, and the complexity of our world. I haven't done enough research regarding this topic, but I know what I feel in a reading and also what the deceased have told me. For the sensitive, empaths, intuitive, and the ones that think they have the gift of mercy, I've put together an outline of each area and you'll see how so many of them overlap or have the same qualities, yet we choose to categorize them with what fits within our ideology. Please note that there's obviously more we can add to this list. However, it's important to see some similarity and to understand the significant differences. I've also made an outline of some of the words I chose to use within this book.

An empath will feel more than a sensitive, intuitive, or even if someone has the gift of mercy. The empath will feel the pain and sickness of others and the spirit world, whereas a sensitive will pick up the energy but won't feel it. It's important to note that being an empath is rarer than most people think it is. I've found certain industries seem to move these words around frequently and inconsistently for their meaning or purpose. An empath definitely experiences more intense emotions than the others. When someone has the gift of mercy they tend to be very emotional and driven towards religion or God in a positive way. However some of their feelings may have a tendency to bring them into areas of religious beliefs that are more intense than others, they'll always come from a place of love and humility. Yet we can see that many overlap and have the same meaning but at a different intensity.

<u>Sensitives:</u>

Overwhelmed easily
Noisy environments affect them easily
Grow angry or 'hangry' when hungry
Over reactive to their bodies in terms of illness or stimulation
Feel uncomfortable when being observed
Feel another people's discomfort
Go into seclusion when overwhelmed
Uncomfortable with loud noises

Susceptible to anxiety and depression
Avoid violence or negative stimulation
More conscientious of their environment
Need time alone
Creative or moved by the arts
Sensitive to nature and animals
Become more emotional at times (over sensitive)
More introverted
Sense when people are lying
Tendency to cling to bitterness

Empaths:

Highly tuned senses (become overwhelmed very easily if not grounded)
Need lots of time alone and avoid being over stimulated
Over stimulation may cause them to become or feel emotional sick
Sensitive to their own biological system
Easily overwhelmed in intimate relationships
Feel other people's pain and illnesses, including the spirit world and animals
Easily overwhelmed with other people's emotions
Highly Intuitive
Highly tuned to noise and smells
Get tired easily
A tendency to give too much
Absorbed other people's emotions when not protected
Often told they are too sensitive
More introverted
Attracted to people in distress
Susceptible to anxiety and depression
Definitely know when people are lying
Troubled by worldly affairs
Feel environmental pain
Must work at forgiveness and positive thoughts daily
Often very misunderstood and taken advantage of

Intuition:

Aware of their emotions
Aware of other people's emotions
Empathic
Self-Aware
Observant
Creative
Play devil's advocate
Tend to over analyze
Both introverted and extraverted and can be both at any given time
Optimistic
Listen to their gut feeling
Known when people are lying
Vivid dreams that can help them with their life questions
Experience deja-vu frequently
Love solitude and don't feel alone

Gift of Mercy:

Kind and gentle
Sense spiritual emotions around them and spirits
Reflect on their spiritual sense
Need to be needed (this is a human condition, but it's really strong here)
Tendency to be introverted
Drawn to sensitive people
Feel they must pray daily
Attracted to people in distress
Embrace humility
Avoid conflict of any kind
Easy to have poor self-image, something we all fight with
Spiritual warrior attitude
Tendency to overly focus on failures
Need to be around positive and trustworthy people
Sense when people are lying but won't always listen to their intuition

The Ego

We all have an ego. It's what drives us to be the best we can be and sometimes the worst we can be. It's in us to help inspire us to live. In our human world we need food, shelter, love, clothing, and health, to name a few, so that we can live within this mortal world. We need none of this in heaven. All is provided to us and all that we need is given within heaven. The ego may have different names and may also be called the shadow self. The ego disappears into the Earth and what we're left with is the remains of pain. The ego isn't a bad thing and we need it. However, it can be overactive, causing havoc within one's life. If the remains are substantial or detrimental, this energy may become residual energy. Not everything is a ghost haunting in your world or homes. Sometimes, they're memories and energy that needs to be healed and dissolved. This can get complicated so I'll leave it here. I want to provide you with an outline of the worlds.

Judgement

Have you heard the comment that God sees everything? Well, he does! The good, the bad and the ugly. In my view, as I said before, He's also a forgiving God and a God of love. He knows his family makes mistakes and He gives us ample opportunity within our lifetime to learn and change, yet many do not. So how does all this work? Well firstly, I should mention that even though God judges, I think we judge ourselves much more negatively and much more harshly than He would, could, or will ever do. That's the way I see it. Judgement doesn't just happen at the end of life and happens during it too. This is why certain things happen in life. I believe God is judging but in such a way that he's trying to put you back on your path. Conflict may be created to give you a wake-up call for you to change your life. Afterlife judgment is different than the physical one. That's where I found that the importance of being a medium fits in. I can talk to the deceased and be the mediator when needed. I can deliver the message from your loved ones so pain can be healed now, with the living.

The Soul

The soul is separate from the ego, which is part of judgment. As I said earlier, the soul leaves the body and goes into heaven while the ego stays, but the ego isn't part of the soul and is only a fragment of the mind. The ego is of the brain. I like to say it's more of the lower self, the place where judgment lays. The ego is vital because it requires us to live life. It gives us drive, makes us want to live our purpose, and propels us forward. However, the ego has a dark side. The dark side is greed, lust, evil desires, the need to be right and justified, the desire to be accepted, and the need for pain. Yes, the need for suffering. Pain keeps us awake. It reminds us we are human and we need to feel pain. When our soul shuts off our mind does the same and we feel empty inside, closed from reality, so we unknowingly search for pain. Within the soul is the true self, the person God intended you to be, but since our mission in life is to learn how to be closer to God and love, we see this love and knowledge as a foreign object and fight it to the bitter end. Why do we do this? It's because we are human. Again, it's what propels us forward to learn. It leads us in a direction that either enlightens us or hinders our purpose. When I worked within the corporate sector, I soon realized that the soul has a purpose for everyone. Some people are afraid of success and they work very hard to ensure that they don't succeed, all while they desire the need for success. It's a little crazy, isn't it? While I'm not going to get into the mechanics of the soul or the soul family within this book as that's enough for an entire other book, what I want to point out is the message of the soul. Your purpose, whatever you decide to choose, comes from your personality. This comes from your desires, which come from the accomplishment your soul needs you to either attain or to overcome. When you learn and accept this, you'll find peace. There's a treasure that sits within you. When you love yourself, you can learn to love others and if you see the truth of God's plan, you'll see that He's already about love. It's our world that creates disharmony, not Him. If you wake up every morning and look at yourself in the mirror and declare that you're perfect and worthy of receiving all the goodness that this world has to offer would you believe it? Not right away because your soul's in pain. It's in pain because of your unhealed lessons and the memories others have instilled within you. Society will constantly remind you that you aren't good enough, that you're not smart enough, not rich enough, or not pretty or handsome enough. You're told this because society wants and needs your pain. Remember, the key to your happiness is within you. You have a choice to believe what truth and reality is.

CHAPTER FOURTEEN

Enhancing The Soul

Our soul carries us into heaven and getting into heaven seems like a straightforward task. However, this isn't the case based on what I've learned and heard from spirit. You might think that following the ten commandments and listening to the teachings of God or just following your good moral instincts is good enough, but is it? I've learned that it's not. At least this is what I've been told from the other side. The worst thing you can do for yourself and your soul is to live your life unforgiven, not necessarily unlived. What do I mean by this? Well, how many times have you moved through life and found yourself angry, focusing on negative past experiences and thoughts, living your life only for today and for you? It's no secret that our world is in pain, but I can see the light that desires to emerge.

I grew up in a time where you could walk down the street and people would smile at a stranger. Today I find it's hard to get a smile out of someone when you're having a happy time walking on a beautiful path outside, even when you're in the mountains, free from environmental stress.

My family and I have created opportunities to make sure we smile and say hello when we're walking on the paths around our city and within the mountains. However, although you'd think this would be an easy task, it's not. I finally had to stop the exertion of trying to smile and say hello to all the by-passers as my kids became sad at how many people didn't say hello back and I was also becoming discouraged. But I told my kids, let's keep pushing forward our smile and hellos might be just what the other individual needs.

Explaining the pain of other people and the importance of keeping true to yourself, even when others don't participate isn't a conversation I wanted to have with my kids. However, I don't want them to grow up in a world where other people try to destroy their happiness. I remember when I ordered a coffee and a treat for my son at a local restaurant. We were excited about this venture. I mean, who isn't when there's chocolate involved? The excitement diminished reasonably quickly when the woman at the counter didn't say hello back when we smiled and said hello. Instead she kept staring at us with a furious expression, which was a little eerie. Neither one of us had ever met or seen her before. It was our first time at that location. After we got our treat, my son asked why she was frowning at us.

"She must be unhappy and having a bad day," I said. "Her actions have nothing to do with you or me. It has everything to do with her."

"Yes, but she smiled at the lady after you," my son said. "I saw and heard her."

"Well, remember we've done nothing wrong," I replied. "For the mistake and pain is within her so try not to have it become within you. Some people pick and choose who they want to smile at and say hello to. They don't know if it's right or wrong, so let's teach them the proper way to be, by being us."

I'm not going to lie. It's hard on some days to say hello and put a smile on your face. I know I'm human too and an empath. You can't desensitize your love for humanity and when you're continuously told during readings how the deceased wanted to live their life better, you can't help but want to make this world a better place too. The dead are always reminding me to be a better person. That's just another reason why I love doing what I do when I'm talking to heaven.

To keep your momentum of happiness, send a prayer for the

people that may have intentionally or unintentionally hurt you, who have caused you harm or discomfort then let God take care of the rest. It does work, but you have to mean it too. If you're being treated poorly somewhere, stay away from that place. Your light or your vibration isn't in alignment with theirs and its causing conflict with your soul. This conflict doesn't mean something is wrong with you or that you did anything wrong, you're just not in line with your values. Instead go to where your comfortable, learn to listen to your intuition, walk away and right out of a place then find another place that makes you feel more at peace if you have to. There are dozens of grocery and coffee shops and you should never give your power away. If you let someone interfere or disrupt your life, you're giving them strength and your soul is becoming disempowered. If your soul stays disempowered for long enough, it makes room for pain, illness, and negative energy to be able to attach itself to your energy field. Now there's one problem with this. What happens when you feel a certain way and perhaps another person doesn't feel the same way as you. Maybe they see things differently than you are seeing? The best answer is go with your gut. Your intuition is for you, and no one has to understand it or go along with it, but if they respect you, they will respect your wishes too, especially when it means a lot to your emotional and physical health.

While being able to speak our truth openly has empowered our world, we must also use caution on how it affects our world and the people in it. We all have a responsibility to the people that are in this world and the planet as a whole. We all share one shared space. Some people feel they can say what they want to say and act negatively at any time with no repercussions, which can cause harm. Hurtful words, gestures, and eye contact can ruin lives and if the person receiving this negativity is having a bad day or is suicidal, mistakes may happen. Suicide is on the rise, angry people are everywhere, but what are we doing about it? If you remain a strong soul, become healthy physically, mentally, emotionally, spiritually, and put on your armour of love I believe you can conquer anything within life. Healthy isn't putting a wall up around your heart and energy field.

That's just another way to allow illness to enter into your soul. Our world is accepting this chaos, but you don't have to and remember that being close to Jesus will help you immensely and you won't know if you don't give Him a try.

Mantra

I have a mantra that I tell my clients to use daily and will share it with you. Put two hands over your heart one above the other, take a deep breath, close your eyes and say these words to yourself.

"I am at peace, I am where I need to be at this moment of time within my life. I am worthy of receiving all the goodness this world has to offer, for I am love. I came from love, I am made of love, I give love, and I will return to love."

As I said before, our primary purpose in this life is to learn how to love. How can we do this when there's been so much pain within our world? I believe there are some things that we can't change in our world, but the human condition requires us to continually try, and that's a good thing. When we see others in pain, the nature of the soul is to help. If we don't then we're failing at the task at hand and your consciousness isn't learning the lesson, which is needed for your soul. Pain is here for us to learn how to love. A healthy soul will feel heartache when they see misfortune. When you're a healthy soul, you naturally want to do better, to see a better world, and this is all very positive. It's one step further for humanity. You take the first step and another will follow.

Moving into a direction that makes you happy and feeling full within your heart and soul is a good thing, but what happens to us when we don't grow, when we don't heal? What happens to our soul? We grieve and our soul grieves with us. This grief makes us feel empty inside, confused and yearning for something more. This is when many people look outside of themselves. They look for either another person or a substance to fill that hole inside them. This is why many people fall into addictions, have extramarital affairs, use people, or only focus on the self instead of being selfless and focusing on others.

Relief for grief

To give you a perfect base of understanding regarding your soul, I want to talk about grief and what it is. In my opinion, grief is the reaction to anything one may have lost that meant something to them. If you think back to everything you've ever lost, that meant something to you, how did you react? How did others react? Loss isn't limited to loss of a loved one. It could be loss of the self, not really knowing who you are, grieving what you want to be, but not knowing how to retrieve or find it. Perhaps you were an only child and missed having a sibling. Maybe you had dreams, hopes, and desires for a brighter or different future. Perhaps you never got the job you wanted or maybe you did then you were let go. How about the people you met in your life where friendship never developed, but you wanted to create that then it ended before its time.

How do you take yourself into the world, once you lost your expectations of what should be? Everyone grieves differently and grief is not limited to one thing. When you pass, you take your soul into the afterlife, which is the real you. Your regrets go with you to heaven, as this is part of your soul lesson. You leave behind the ego, which has been recreated many times, depending on what you've experienced within this lifetime. Ego carries anger, negatively anything that's in opposition to the light. When we allow our mind, body, and actions to remain in alignment with the light, our soul is in alignment with truth. Throughout this book, I've written about heaven and the reality that life lives on even after death. In fact, death doesn't exist at all, only the death of the physical body. I spoke about what your deceased loved ones desire for you while you're alive on this planet. I know grief is painful. I've gone through it too, but grief is different for everyone. Grief has no ending, it only gets better with time, and your pain will eventually move into memories, hopefully happy ones. This is the biggest and loudest message the deceased have said to me.

"Live your life with happiness, fulfill your time here on Earth with purpose and be the best person you can be. One that's pleasing to God, for He too watches over you waiting and wanting you to realize that life is a gift. Life gives you the foundation that's needed for the next one, life within His kingdom".

CHAPTER FIFTEEN

Forgiveness

I want to provide you with a forgiveness technique that may help you on your journey. Forgiveness is one of the layers we need to peel back so we can reach the light that's within our soul.

Forgiveness is the first and most vital step in any spiritual healing or healing practice of any kind. We must learn to love all with our hearts. This doesn't mean that we accept what the other has done, but we acknowledge the hurt, acknowledge that your ego is only trying to protect you and that's why you feel what you feel. Your gratitude list will correspond with this forgiveness portion, if you desire. After you've made your gratitude list for a person you need to heal through, I want you to compare it with the person you are needing to forgive. This means that your gratitude list may also be about the person you need to forgive. And maybe one of the people you need to forgive is yourself. I also want to mention that when you come to think about why they did this, you need to remember that some people aren't well. Some aren't aware of morals or carry empathy within them. You might think they should know what they did was wrong, but the truth is that maybe they didn't know and you must accept this. When people inflict pain on you, it's not about you, it's about them. Something deep within them is in pain and causing confusion and conflict within their soul, allowing them to act out the pain on another. It seems to release their pain for a while, only to drive them deeper into more depression. It's a cycle and this that can be broken, with help.

When we look at what you may have gained through the experience, I don't want you to sit within your pain. I want you to take the pain and turn it into a gift. Did the pain make you stronger? How? Who did you become from the pain? Is who you are valuable to yourself or another? Can you use this and turn it into a gift that helps another? Through our pain, we learn to help another through their grief. What did you learn? Did you learn whether your pain made you into a better person? Have you learned through your pain how not to be and how to shed more light into this world? These are all valuable life lessons, no matter how you look at it. Don't remain the victim. Become the survivor that turns into a warrior of light and love. After you've written this out in point form, I want you to write a letter, which you'll address to the individual you're writing to.

You'll start with your pain, so write out how you feel and get angry if needed. In the second part you add gratitude. Here's an example.

"(Person) I'm angry at you for leaving this relationship. You asked me to marry you then you leave with no real explanation only for me to see you with another person one week later. How could you? Didn't you love me or love what we had? I'm angry at you, not to mention devastated. I don't think I'll ever love again and this is all your fault. You deserve what you get and I hope your relationship goes sour and that I'm there to see it."

Now here's another example of a paragraph containing gratitude and forgiveness.

"Dear (person), I'm working through the pain I feel regarding our recent breakup. I feel taken advantage of and lied to, as I thought we were in love. I understand you have a new relationship and wish you all the best. As I look back at our relationship, I realize you wanted out a long time ago. You couldn't speak your truth about us.

Looking back, I see you may have an addiction to relationships and don't like being alone and I now see this has been a theme within your love relationships. However, I'm also noticing that there's a theme with me. I seem to attract love relationships where I'm the giver and the other person is the taker. I knew you weren't happy, but I felt I could make you happy and this didn't leave me satisfied either. I can see now that our breakup has been a blessing in disguise as it's now allowing me to work through my issues that I need to heal so that I can attract the right person into my life. I hope you get the opportunity to do the same and not continue with your destructive ways. I'm ready to move on. I forgive you, and I thank God for giving me the right opportunity to receive true happiness. I'm excited about what the future will bring me.

Gratitude list regarding (person):

I experienced love
I learned about myself
I learned about the importance of being truthful
I learned about balance within relationships
I am learning to stand up for myself
I realize I'm stronger than I thought I was
I'm learning about the importance of pain
I'm learning to grieve and understand the importance of it
For the first time I'm realizing what type of relationship I truly need in my life.
I think you're getting the idea about the gratitude. You can go even deeper with this.
Your mind remembers and your soul feels when you manually write it out. Begin your outline and then write your letter.
Who is the first person you'd like to forgive:
What did they do to you?
How did it make you feel?
Why do you think they did this?
Did you learn something from this experience?
Is there a second person? If so, keep going, since you need to do

this for everyone that may have hurt you in your life or to the people that you need to forgive.

Affirmation for forgiveness

Say this affirmation daily as you're working through forgiveness. "I acknowledge my fear and anger. I understand that my soul is only trying to protect me. I'm a healthy, beautiful, and powerful person and am learning to forgive. I'm working at moving forward within my life."

White-light protection

Before any prayer of forgiveness or before the last step after writing the letter, I want you to do a white light protection for yourself. White light protection is always essential. I think of this as prayer. I'm asking God to provide me with His seal of protection to contain and protect the light that's within me. Visualize beautiful bright light coming down from the heavens, going through the crown of your head and down to your toes. Take a nice deep breath and feel the warm energy flowing through your feet, up your legs, thighs, stomach, chest, arms, back, neck, throat, face, and beaming all around and within you. This white light is there to protect you from negativity and any harm you've experienced in your past. I call upon the power and the love of Jesus to help release my pain and help me replace it with forgiveness within my heart.

Prayer

Jesus with your help I release all fear and anger from (put in person or situation). I now give it to you, Jesus. Please release me from any negative thoughts, feelings, and images I may have from this (circumstance and person.) Jesus, please take away my pains of energy and replace it with your grace.

Final step

You have done your letter, you have set the white light protection to yourself, you have invoked the prayer, and now you're ready to burn the letter in a fire-safe bowl outside. Your words will enter into heaven and allow God's angels to place them where needed.

Closing step

Whenever you ask for help from the spiritual realm you must always close it with a thank you prayer.

"Lord, thank you for giving me this opportunity to grow. I now release (put in personal names or situation) from me and I send the words of healing into the universe for you to take them away from me, for this I give thanks. Amen."

You can use this for any circumstance from which you may need healing. It's also a great time to do this on the night of a new moon.

Other forgiveness techniques

Visualize Jesus in front of you after you white light protect yourself. See the person or the circumstance that you need to forgive. Jesus gives you a beautiful, sizeable pink ball of light. You'll visualize the pain or the adverse situation you experienced to enter into this pink ball of light, which contains the hurt this person inflicted on you. You're going to give this pink ball of light back to Jesus.

"Jesus, I release all fears, worries and anger regarding (put in a person's name or situation). I release this to you to heal. I give thanks and thank you for all your help. Amen."

Other prayers

Visualize pink energy flowing into your heart and this energy is coming directly from the divine, God or His angels, whatever brings you comfort.

"I ask that you help me remove any negative energy or thoughts from my heart. I'm working towards forgiveness so that I can shine my light on this world. I ask for your assistance and love to help me gain the knowledge, healing, and strength needed within my heart, so I may be able to move forward with my life peacefully. For this, I give thanks, Amen."

I also wanted to provide you with a form I developed called the Circle of Healing. This form is to keep you on track with your life, to help you move forward. I also believe that Sunday is a time of rest and is essential for the soul.

The Circle of Healing

Every circumstance is a gift that will help you move forward in life.

	MONDAY	TUESDAY	WEDNESDAY	THURSDAY	FRIDAY	SATURDAY	SUNDAY
Gratitude							
Affirmation							
Mantra							
Self-Love Mantra/Pray							
Journaling							
Life Contribution							
Forgiveness							
Positive Self-Talk							

The meaning of each daily task

Within every journey of personal development, healing, and spiritual growth, one must start with some specific tasks. The journey of healing starts with forgiveness, or forgiving yourself and others. This is different for everyone. The journey of raising your vibrations and clearing your energy field begins by following through with specific tasks that will not only raise your energetic vibrational frequency but also help with clearing the emotional body too.

You must make sure that each one of these tasks are done daily and each time you complete this task you will put a check mark in each one of these boxes. There should be one check mark for the mantra, the journaling, and the affirmation. The rest of the boxes should have at least two check marks.

Let's just say that more is better and you'll move forward with your healing and your life quicker.

Please remember, I want you to add quality check marks, meaning that you really made an effort to move forward with this task. Eventually you will become so good at it that the process will be a natural way of being!

Gratitude

Being grateful for your life, a situation, a decision, people within your life, those that have been in your life, or your past experiences, in short anything you can dream up that puts you in a state of gratitude.

Self-love

Loving yourself. What do you do every day that says, I love myself? A list of possibilities could include:

- Your mantra
- Your affirmation
- Taking a walk
- Buying something you love or buying a gift for another

- Saving for something you love
- Reading a book that you love
- Daily meditation or prayer
- Yoga or working out
- Taking time and honoring the mind, body, and soul

Journaling

This needs to be done every night or whenever it fits into your daily schedule. This type of journaling is done a specific way. Please write out your feelings and emotions for the day. Look at what your experience was and what you were feeling. I want you to 'see' the lesson brought forth or 'see' what needs to be cleared then look for the blessings within the situation. There's a blessing in every circumstance. It's how we view the situation that determines whether it's changeable or not.

Life contribution

This could be a big one for many people. This is also the one task that will put you into the seat of happiness quickly.

- Help others
- Say hello to someone you meet or have made eye contact with
- Say hello to a stranger
- Always saying thank you
- Acknowledging other people's accomplishments
- Compliment other people
- Donate to a charity
- Say I love you to someone you love
- Give a hug a day (animals and trees count too)
- Do something nice for someone (this could be intertwined with other tasks)
- Pray for others
- Visualize positive images going into our world or to others

Positive self-talk

- Your mantra
- Say you love yourself
- Congratulate yourself on a job well done
- Be aware of the words you speak as words hold energy
- Say I look good today and mean it
- Remember that you are what you think you are

Forgiveness

- Forgive others for what they have done or said
- Forgive yourself for anything that may have caused a disturbance in your life or in the lives of others
- Forgiveness exercise

There are no coincidences and nothing happens by chance. You are the creator in your life and you can design it any way you want. You need to believe in yourself, your life, our Creator, and the universe.

Everything that has happened has done so by design. Seek the lesson within each circumstance and learn from it. This will release you from many life contracts or negative attachments! When you become at peace with yourself, you obtain the opportunity to increase your natural born intuitive abilities. A calm mind and an open heart can reach into the spiritual realm much more easily than a busy and angry one can.

CHAPTER SIXTEEN

~

Some Final Words

Thank you for being on this journey with me. I'll continue on my journey and seek truth, where truth is needed. The light I spoke of and the experiences I endured earlier in this book were a preparation that my soul was to experience. It was one that I needed to have for my heart to become one with the light.

I'm honoured to be in service to the living, to your departed loved ones, and to God. I never consider mediumship as a talent. Being a medium is a spiritual gift that can help many people. It's essential to explain why I call this a gift. My ability to talk to the other side is here to help other people heal. Through God, I serve as a gateway for heaven to help you and the deceased heal. This ability isn't for me but for you and that is a gift.

Every time I do a reading, I'm humbled. Your loved ones share so much with me. They tell me about their life, your life, and healing. Through my deep connection, I feel their love, personality, soul, and even their pain. Sometimes there are no words that allow me to express the gratitude I feel for what I do.

When I do a reading, it's you, me, and your loved ones all sitting down together and having a conversation. While your loved ones bring through their personality and characteristics, I always strive to make sure you receive all the validation you need. In reality, I communicate what they tell me. This includes how they passed, how they look, their names or names within the family, what they did in the physical world, their memories, struggles, and life lessons. I'll always share any information they want to tell you, information that helps you heal.

I think it's essential to let you know that I'll always be a follower of Jesus Christ. No one can take that away from me and no one can take that away from you. I'm not afraid to tell this world that I believe and neither should you. Even though I'm a believer in Jesus Christ, I don't expect others to be or do the same.

I look forward to where He takes me on this beautiful journey we call life and will surrender to whatever the calling is, with Him. Even though I have spoken about evil with this book, I do believe that for many if evil enters into one's life, it must be a choice. That I have experienced. Sometimes evil enters into someone's life without them even knowing it, causing, pain, conflict, and discomfort to their life and soul. I've learned that if you live your life with God first and with love second, His truth will show you the way. I want to share with you some words that spirit has told me.

"Life is like a painting. You have the ability to change the colours and the pictures of your past, your present, and your future, by how you view it. In your painting, you can put happiness or you can put sadness. The choice is yours. I gave you a canvas and whatever picture you decide to choose to paint, I will love. For when we see each other again, which won't be for a long time, I expect to see many paintings because I didn't give you one canvas to paint, I gave you many."

My dedication

I dedicate this book to those that are grieving and for those that feel different as a medium, psychic, sensitive, intuitive, and an empath. I also dedicate this book to all the souls that now watch over us from heaven, to my wonderful husband, my two beautiful boys and the souls that have chosen me to be an ambassador of their word. Thank you.

The dead should never be forgotten, as that was never God's intention. I will strive to tell their stories and be the voice of truth and love for all of our dearly departed.
God Bless!

Manufactured by Amazon.ca
Bolton, ON

23569044R00097